GW01100073

The art of cuisine lies in allowing the food to taste of itself.

Curnonsky

Gero Hottinger
Kaj G. Lindholm
Pekka Råman

Simply delicious!
Pure Finnish Flavours

Otava Publishing Company, Helsinki

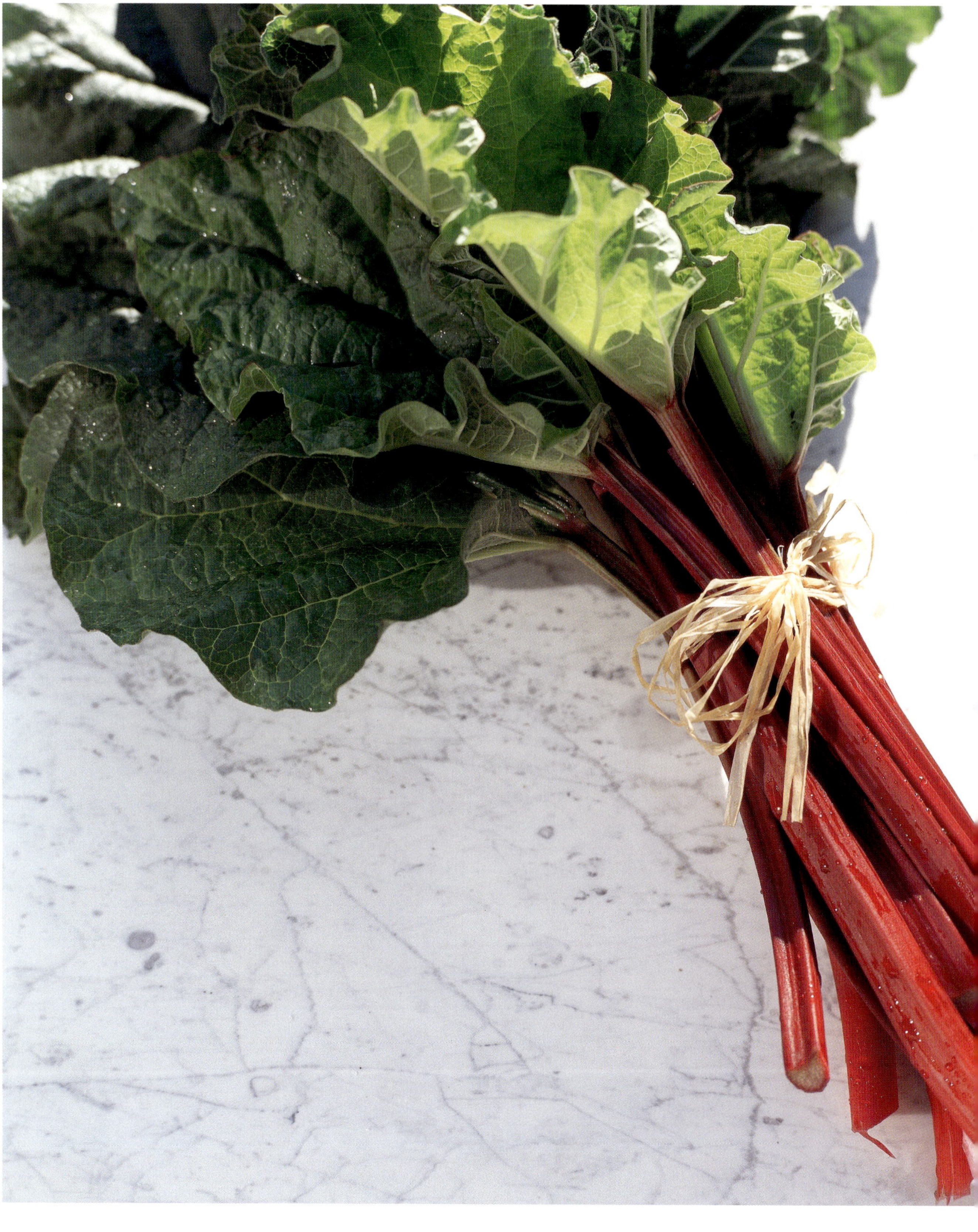

Contents

Gero Hottinger, master chef ... 7
The Savoy Hotel, Düsseldorf, on April Fools' Day, 1964 ... 9
"No, no, Mr. Hottinger! That's not how you peel asparagus!" ... 11

Starters ... 12

"Do you know, Mr. Hottinger, what Forelle Blau is?" ... 13
Lutefisk and glassmaster's herring ... 15
Wondrous are the delicacies of gentlemen! ... 19
Life in the land of salt and allspice ... 27
The mother of a new, more cheerful style of restaurant ... 28
Mascarpone in my suitcase ... 30
Ville de Paris and his salmon soup ... 35

Soups ... 36

Fish courses ... 46

The Marshal of Finland and a German chef – at the same restaurant, but at different times ... 55

Something green ... 72

Meat dishes ... 78

Two cooks on the waterfront ... 83
"If only it were as much fun as this in every school!" ... 93
"Restaurant of the Year" after four years in business ... 102
Not just any hamburger steak ... 106
A time – and a place – for everything ... 111

Desserts ... 114

The unforgettable tart ... 123
Spring comes to the innkeeper ... 127
"Gero, tell us the proper way to plan a menu" ... 129
Cooking is a matter of skill, not of equipment ... 132
The false morel, Gyromitra esculenta.
How to handle this poisonous mushroom ... 134
Weights, Measures & Temperatures ... 135
Our warmest thanks ... 136
Sources ... 137
Index to the recipes ... 138

SIMPLY DELICIOUS!

Gero Hottinger, master chef

GERO HOTTINGER CAME TO FINLAND over thirty years ago. He was born in Düsseldorf, Germany, in 1948 and began his culinary career as a 16-year-old apprentice in the kitchens of that city's Savoy Hotel.

After qualifying as a chef, he spent some years at the Kurhotel Atlantic in Baden-Baden, until he resolved in 1969 to fulfil his boyhood dream of travelling to Scandinavia. His journey took him to the celebrated Grand Hôtel in Stockholm and from there to Finland.

He became familiar with the kitchens of many of the finest hotels and restaurants in Helsinki in the course of the following decades, including Kalastajatorppa, the Rivoli, the Palace Hotel's La Vista and the Savoy, and in 1994 he was instrumental in founding the Kanavaranta Restaurant and the Helsinki Culinary Institute, Finland's first school of haute cuisine.

GERO IS ALSO WELL-KNOWN as one of Finland's first TV cooks, and he has done much to spread knowledge of Finnish gastronomy and cooking abroad, arranging Finnish Food Weeks in countries such as Japan, Iceland, Italy and Germany. Nowadays he runs the Helsinki Culinary Institute and the Villa Hakkari manor house restaurant in Lempäälä, which was opened in Spring 2004.

The brigade of chefs at the Savoy Hotel, Düsseldorf, in spring 1964. The Oberküchenmeister, Leo Gillrath, is seated on the left, and the apprentice Gero Hottinger is the second from the right on the back row. Young apprentice cooks were so slim in those days!

The Savoy Hotel, Düsseldorf, on April Fools' Day, 1964

AT LAST PRACTICALLY A YEAR as the hotel's piccolo is over! There the slim-faced young apprentice cook stands in the middle of the vast kitchens in his brand new chef's coat and apron stretching almost down to the ground, ready at the ripe age of 16 to take on the whole culinary world.

In vain had the Herr Oberküchenmeister tried to convince me a year earlier of the less desirable aspects of the profession – the arduous work, the long days that seem as if they will never end, and the uncongenial working hours.

In those days the kitchens of a big hotel would have twenty or more professionals buzzing around, from the buffet chef to the pâtissier, and a few apprentices whose sacrifice on the altar of the culinary arts was to do most of the menial tasks, from potato peeling to washing the saucepans.

The daily routine began early in the morning, and if the master chef thought you were looking too eager to make for home by the afternoon, he might very well suggest that in future you could stay there, since you seemed to like home so much!

ONCE A WEEK THERE WAS formal instruction, during which the apprentices studied in theory more or less all the things that they were in any case to learn by practical experience over the years.

Three months on salads, three months on meats, three months on fish and three months on soups and sauces – and then back to salads again: the apprentice's life was a simple one, although by no means an easy one. With each cycle you nevertheless felt that you knew a little more than the last time – and at least a little more than the newcomers who had been taken on in the meantime.

THE APPRENTICESHIP LASTED THREE YEARS, and ended with the examination, which according to the rules had to be taken at another restaurant.

Three years earlier I had applied for an apprenticeship in the restaurant of the Breidenbacher Hof hotel, which I regarded as the best in the whole of Düsseldorf, but I was turned down, so I was highly delighted when they agreed to take me for my examination.

My examination piece in all its splendour, on a silver platter at the Breidenbacher Hof. Full marks except for a small error: I had arranged the slices of roast pork on the dish with the fatty edge downwards, an inexcusable slip that could perhaps be blamed in this case on stage-fright!

SIMPLY DELICIOUS!

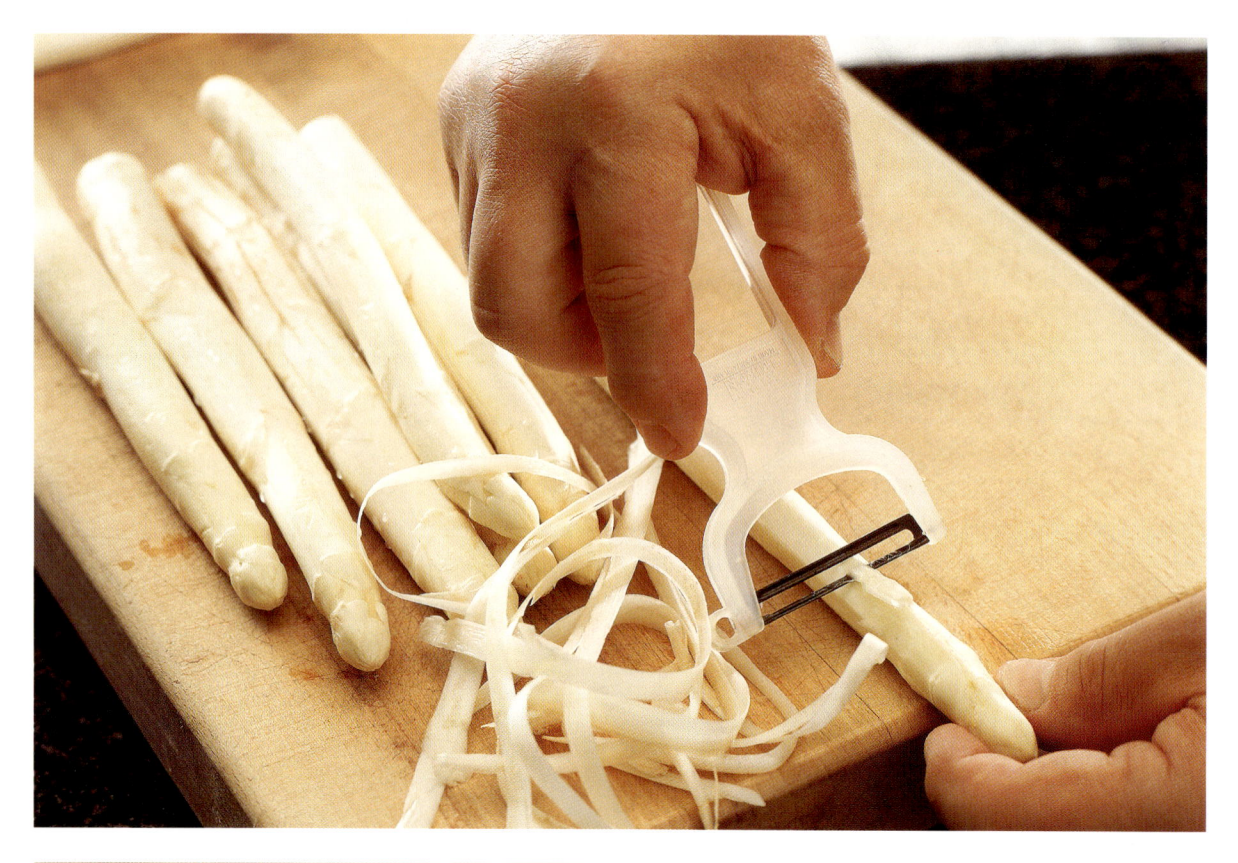

"No, no, Mr. Hottinger! That's not how you peel asparagus!"

I HAD JUST HAD THE FIRST promotion in my career, to study the art of cold dishes in the fantastical world of salads and vegetables. I was no longer "Young man" but "Mr. Hottinger"! Before me was a bowl of fresh white asparagus, freshly picked that morning, and in my hand was a proper peeler. I had peeled asparagus before, of course, so I knew how to do it.

The expression on Herr Oberküchenmeister's face nevertheless told me that things had not entirely gone as they should. Was my magnificently successful career about to end in an ignominious belly-flop?

Leo Gillrath was a massive and impressive figure, and he took the stick of asparagus and the knife from my mildly quivering fingers, laid the asparagus gently on the formidable palm of his hand with the tip pointing forwards, took up the knife like a conductor does his baton and with elegant strokes began to shave the thinnest of strips perfectly evenly off the stick of asparagus, working from the lower edge of the tip down towards the base.

"Like this, Mr. Hottinger, lightly, like the best of shaves. Not too much and not too little. Verstanden?"

PROFESSIONAL CHEFS who have to peel hundreds of sticks of asparagus a day at the height of the season manage to do it without breaking scarcely any of them, by following this well-tried method:

Set the sticks of asparagus out side by side on a good-sized chopping board with the tips pointing to the left (if you are right-handed) and projecting far enough over the edge of the board that you can easily take hold of the stem with your thumb and forefinger. Then just let fly with the peeler!

If the asparagus is freshly picked that day the outer skin will peel off in very thin strips, but if it has been stored for longer you will have to press a little harder.

Finally cut away the dry part at the base of each stick, leaving them all the same length.

Some people like the taste of green asparagus with its peel, but I would always peel that, too, however young and fresh it might be.

COOKING ASPARAGUS is a simple matter. An actual asparagus pan is an amusing thing, of course, but by no means an essential. Asparagus will cook just as well lying flat in a shallow saucepan.

Put the peeled sticks into boiling salt water and add a couple of lumps of sugar, as this will set the asparagus laughing and take away its natural, slightly bitter aftertaste! Leave it to simmer for about 8 minutes, poking it with the tip of a knife from time to time to check how it's softening. Lift it out of the saucepan and leave it to rest for a moment, preferably wrapped in a clean teatowel.

Asparagus with puff pastries and orange zabaglione

To serve 4 persons

2 bunches of white asparagus
prepared choux pastry

For the zabaglione
   3 egg yolks
   1 dl orange juice
   4 cl Noilly Prat vermouth
   20 g fructose
   3 tbsp sour cream or whipped cream
   salt and freshly ground white pepper

For the puff pastries Roll out the pastry to a thickness of 5 mm and cut it into good-sized triangles.

Mix an egg yolk with a little water and brush onto the top surfaces of the triangles.

Bake the triangles in a 190°C oven for about 14 mins and allow to cool.

Meanwhile cook the asparagus in water flavoured with salt and sugar (for instructions, see p. 11).

For the zabaglione Strain the orange juice and mix it with the vermouth, egg yolks and sugar in a saucepan. Beat the mixture over hot but not boiling water until it thickens.

Add the sour cream or whipped cream. Season with salt and pepper to taste.

Divide the asparagus sticks out onto plates, pour the sauce onto them and place a puff pastry on top of each helping.

"Do you know, Mr. Hottinger, what Forelle Blau is?"

OF COURSE MR. HOTTINGER KNEW! Fortunately he had practiced with the recipe for this speciality from Baden-Baden, north-eastern France and Austria in his home kitchens at the Savoy Hotel.

"Then it's agreed that Mr. Hottinger will take care of today's trout", the officious master chef of Baden-Baden's finest spa hotel announced with no further ceremony to the new under-chef shortly after he had arrived there.

Unfortunately, Forelle Blau, or Truites au Bleu, as the French call it, will not work with Finnish brown trout, as it requires trout from the mountain streams of Central Europe. But even though you are not able to prepare this delicacy at home, you may be interested in knowing how it gains its fine deep-blue colour.

THE CORRECT WAY to prepare Forelle Blau is to take a living trout of a suitable size for one portion out of the water and kill it 10 mins before it is to be cooked. Open it up and clean it quickly, without wiping or rinsing it. Then immerse it in a court-bouillon, a stock strongly seasoned with wine vinegar together with carrot, onion, bay leaves, stems of parsley, salt and whole white peppers.

Cook the fish in this stock for 6–7 mins and then pour off the liquid carefully and serve with melted butter and grated horseradish or with hollandaise sauce.

I CAN'T REMEMBER how many trout were prepared like this in the kitchens of the Kurhotel Atlantic in Baden-Baden, but it was one of the most popular luncheon dishes of all. The elegant and affluent guests at the spa were in any case treated to nothing but the best in all gastronomic matters – wild boar, deer, elk, pheasant, hare, and so on. And all these came straight from local suppliers!

Everything was prepared on the spot from the basic ingredients: the birds were plucked and hung, the game animals were cut up and whole fish were cleaned and filleted in the restaurant's own kitchens.

Young chefs could scarcely hope for an education like that anywhere nowadays, unfortunately.

Finnish charr au bleu

To serve 4 persons

1 whole charr, cleaned, weighing about 600–800 g
kitchen thread for tying up
about 3 l water
2 bay leaves
1 small onion or piece of leek
10 whole white peppers
1 dl white wine vinegar
1.5 dl sea salt

For the horseradish sauce

2 dl whipped cream
freshly grated horseradish to taste
white wine vinegar
sugar

Many people think of the charr as a difficult fish to cook because of its idiosyncratic taste, and perhaps it is indeed at its best when simply fried in butter, either whole or filleted, but it also provides an interesting gastronomic experience when boiled whole in this fashion, and as such is eminently suitable as a warm starter or a light main course. It does not change colour as a trout does, but the overall impression is pleasing enough for anyone who has tasted Forelle Blau at some time.

Tie the neck and tail of the charr together to form a loose ring that will fit into your saucepan more easily.

When the water is boiling, add the sliced onion and all the other seasoning and allow these to boil together for a moment, then reduce the heat and lower the fish gently into the water, taking care not to break its skin.

Meanwhile mix the whipped cream and grated horseradish to the strength that you prefer and season this with a drop of wine vinegar and a sprinkling of sugar.

When the fish is cooked, lift it carefully out of the stock with a large skimming ladle, divide it into portions and serve with boiled potatoes, for instance.

Lutefisk and glassmaster's herring

WHEN I CAME TO SCANDINAVIA in 1969 I knew very little about the area, even less about Sweden and practically nothing about Finland, but I had been dreaming for years about the unspoiled nature in the region, the forests, sparkling waters and the salmon, whitefish and perch swimming in them. One day I had to come and see and experience all this, and now this day had dawned, so "Skandinavien – Ich bin unterwegs!"

In fact a friend and I had applied for jobs on the M/S Gripsholm, flagship of the Svenska-Amerika Lines that sailed between Gothenburg and New York and was one of the most stylish ocean liners of its day. More than the ship or the port of Gothenburg, however, we were fascinated by the prospect of seeing the New World, and we had already decided to try our luck in the land of the Golden Dollar.

And it very nearly turned out that way. Our application was accepted, but the reply from the shipping company arrived a fraction too late. We had already accepted jobs at the Grand Hôtel in Stockholm, which we had regarded as a good second choice. So it was goodbye to ideas of the Atlantic Ocean, Gothenburg and the west coast of Sweden.

But there are fish swimming in the Baltic Sea, too, as we soon found out.

> The first question was
> "Where are the great Swedish chefs?"

The cramped, labyrinthine kitchens of the Grand Hôtel were teeming with almost a hundred cooks every day, but apart from the cold table chefs, they all seemed to be "immigrants" like us. Perhaps the most revered chef in Sweden at that time was the legendary master chef of the Operakällaren restaurant and caterer to the royal household, Werner Vögeli, and he hailed from Emmental in Switzerland!

The situation nowadays is quite different. There are dozens of top chefs from Sweden, many with worldwide reputations, and not least among their Finnish colleagues.

BUT SWEDISH HUSMANSKOST tastes of Swedish husmanskost whatever language it is in. Traditional home cooking was a firm favourite with the aristocratic gentlemen who lunched at the Grand Hôtel, and we were initiated into the hidden secrets of the national culinary heritage with typical Swedish efficiency and gentle determination even though the only language we had in common was often kitchen French.

I fell inescapably in love with many dishes whose names I couldn't even pronounce at first, but you can imagine how happy I was when I came across the same delicacies in Finland. And again I couldn't pronounce their names: *lasimestarin silli, paistettuja silakoita etikkaliemessä, lihapullia, kaalikääryleitä, kraavilohta ja sinappi- kastiketta, kermamuhennettuja kantarelleja ja uusia perunoita,* in other words glassmaster's herring, fried Baltic herrings in a vinegar marinade, meat balls, cabbage rolls, fresh salmon with mustard sauce and chopped chanterelles in a cream sauce with new potatoes.

Plaited herring with a sour cream and apple sauce

To serve 4 persons

4 evenly sized fillets of matjes herring

For the sauce
6 dl sour cream
1 onion
2 apples
2 pickled cucumbers
2 bay leaves
salt and freshly ground white pepper
a little chives
some sprigs of dill

Peel the onion and the apples. Cut the onion into thin slices and the apples into thin pieces. Cut and slice the pickled cucumbers.

Mix all the ingredients together and season with salt and freshly ground white pepper. Add the bay leaves and allow to stand overnight in a cold place.

Cut the herring fillets into three lengthways, leaving the strips attached to each other slightly at the tail end. Plait the strips as you would a loaf of coffee bread.

Form the sour cream and apple sauce into a neat pyramid on the plate and arrange the plaited herring on top. Garnish with finely chopped chives and sprigs of dill.

Whitefish tartare flavoured with gin

To serve 4 persons

600 g boned whitefish fillets
1 shallot
dill
1 tbsp coarse Dijon mustard
8 crushed juniper berries
8 cl gin
salt and freshly ground white pepper

Carefully bone the fish, cut the fillets into thin slices and divide these into small pieces.

Chop the shallot and the dill.

Mix all the ingredients together into a smooth paste, add the gin and allow to stand in the fridge for about an hour.

Form the paste into four equal-sized cakes and garnish with slices of sweet pepper or sprigs of dill, for instance. Serve with toasted rye bread.

Smoked Baltic herring salad

To serve 4 persons

- 12 whole Baltic herrings, smoked
- 2–3 kinds of lettuce (e.g. plain, curled or endive)
- 1 red pepper
- 3 small tomatoes
- 200 g champignons
- 4 spring onion stems
- 4 radishes

For the salad dressing
- 2 dl crème fraîche
- 2 fresh sprigs of tarragon
- 1 tbsp finely chopped parsley
- 1 tsp finely chopped dill
- 1 tsp finely chopped basil
- salt and freshly ground white pepper

Remove the skins from the Baltic herrings and clean them carefully so that the fillets remain intact.

Rinse all the salad ingredients well.

Chop the red pepper, tomatoes, champignons and radishes into thin slices and the spring onion stems into rings. Mix together in a salad bowl and place the cleaned Baltic herring fillets on top.

To prepare the salad dressing Stir the finely chopped herbs into the crème fraîche and season with salt and pepper. Pour the dressing over the salad or serve separately.

Wondrous are the delicacies of gentlemen!

BOX UPON BOX of the finest fish that the rivers and lakes of the north had to offer passed through the kitchens of the Grand Hotel in those days: salmon from Swedish Lapland, cod, turbot and prawns from the west coast, perch and pike-perch from the Swedish lakes and eels and plaice from the Straits of Denmark.

At lunchtime a huge table with Baltic herring prepared in at least twenty different ways would be laid out on the Veranda, the restaurant's glassed-in terrace, and the selection would be varied from day to day.

For a young, enthusiastic junior cook this was marvellous, as was the delight shown by distinguished Swedish visitors with the authentically prepared traditional dishes. I remember almost thinking aloud to myself on one occasion, "Oh, Mother! Your son has certainly come a long way. Here he is, standing in the kitchens of the most magnificent hotel in the whole of Scandinavia frying Baltic herring for Prince Bertil of Sweden!"

BUT AS CHRISTMAS APPROACHED the boxes of fresh fish began to be interspersed more and more often with other, odd-looking boxes of dried fish, which were immediately rushed down to the cellar, where their obnoxious-smelling contents were tipped out into huge tubs of water to soak. There these wizened fillets of cod and haddock gradually softened and swelled to a translucent mass that was to my mind quite amazing to behold.

You can imagine my astonishment, then, when just before Christmas this travesty of a fish in a muslin bag was served up with boiled potatoes, peas and béchamel sauce at a rate of several hundred portions a day – and to the hotel's very best clients at that!

I was still unaware then that this same lutfisk is a great Christmas delicacy for the Finns as well.

Finland and Sweden have been engaged since the beginnings of time in a never-ending series of international matches in practically every field of life, but there is one discipline in which the Swedes come out as victors by a clear margin of 2–0, and that is the slicing of salted or smoked salmon. This is because they begin at the thick end of the fillet, so that they get more beautiful big slices out of it than the Finns, who begin at the tail. It also means that the Finns have more little pieces left over, although they have admittedly learned to dispose of them ingeniously in an utterly delicious salmon casserole with sliced potato, eggs, cream and chopped dill.

Vegetable terrine with fresh tomato sauce

For the terrine

    small florets of cauliflower
    small florets of broccoli
    1 x 1 cm cubes of carrot
    whole green beans, or
    1 x 1 cm cubes of celery
    (equal quantities of each, to a total volume of
    1–1.2 l when diced)

    2 tbsp finely chopped parsley
    2 tbsp finely chopped dill
    water
    salt
    3 dl crème fraîche
    10 leaves of gelatine

For the tomato sauce:

    3 tomatoes
    1 dl tomato juice
    3 sprigs of basil
    3 sprigs of parsley
    salt and freshly ground white pepper

To prepare the terrine Boil the diced vegetables in mildly salted water until just cooked al dente. Lift them out directly into cold water to cool and then pour all the water off. Save the water in which they were cooked as a stock.

Mix the crème fraîche into 7 dl of this stock, add the chopped herbs, bring to the boil and check the amount of salt.

Soak the gelatine leaves in cold water for 10 mins, squeeze the water out carefully and add the leaves to the hot stock, stirring all the time. Cool to room temperature.

Mix the vegetables together and place them in a rectangular terrine dish. Pour the stock over them and leave in a cool place for a day to set.

To prepare the sauce Scald the tomatoes, remove the seeds and cut the tomatoes into pieces. Put all the ingredients in a blender and reduce to a pulp.

Sieve the resulting pulp and season with salt and white pepper.

To serve, dip the dish in hot water first so that the terrine will slide out more easily. Then turn the terrine out onto a chopping board and cut it into slices about 1 cm thick.

Spread tomato sauce on a plate and put a slice of terrine on top.

Warm chanterelle salad and balsámico syrup

To serve 4 persons

300 g small chanterelles
8 radishes
1 lettuce
1 lollo rosso lettuce
1 curled lettuce
2 tomatoes
3 tbsp shelled walnuts
120 g bacon
30 g butter for frying
salt and freshly ground white pepper

For the salad dressing
1 dl olive oil
0.5 dl balsámico vinegar
a little sea salt and white pepper from a mill

For the balsámico syrup
1 dl balsámico vinegar
0.25 dl soy sauce
60 g caster sugar

First prepare the balsámico syrup.

Put all the ingredients in a saucepan and boil until the liquid has thickened to a pliable syrup. Take it off the heat and allow to cool.

Clean the chanterelles and rinse the lettuces. Scald the tomatoes, remove the seeds and slice.

Cut the radishes in half and then into thin slices.

Cut the bacon into small pieces and fry them in a dry pan until crisp. Lift them out into a sieve and allow any extra fat to drain off. Fry the chanterelles in a little butter at first, until the liquid coming from them has evaporated, then add more butter and fry them until done. Season them with salt and white pepper.

Tear the lettuce leaves into pieces and place in a bowl. Add the slices of tomato and radish.

Mix the salad dressing ingredients together well. Pour onto the salad and mix.

Draw fancy patterns on the plates with the syrup, serve out portions of salad and decorate them with the chanterelles, bacon and chopped walnuts.

Duck's liver hamburger

To serve 4 persons

8 slices of toast bread
1–2 large apples
4 slices of fresh duck's liver, altogether about 300 g
butter for frying
sea salt and freshly ground white pepper

Peel and core the apple(s). Cut into 8 rings about 5 mm thick.

Toast the slices of bread and fry the apple rings in butter. Then fry the duck's liver in a hot pan and season with sea salt and pepper.

Build the ingredients into a hamburger. Garnish it with chervil or parsley and the plate with balsámico syrup made according to the recipe on p. 23.

Soufflé of potato, boletus mushrooms and quark

To serve 6 persons

6 soufflé dishes
160 g floury potatoes
60 g melted butter
6 eggs
150 g quark
a little sugar
1 tsp white truffle oil
100 g finely chopped, cooked boletus mushrooms
soft butter and flour to line the dishes

For the sauce
300 g diced boletus mushrooms
1 shallot
1.5 dl sour cream
0.5 dl whipping cream
20 g butter
salt and white pepper

Cook the potatoes and mash them through a fine sieve while still hot. Add the melted butter and mix gently.

Mix the quark and egg yolks together well and add to the mashed potatoes. Add a little sugar and the white truffle oil.

Sauté the mushrooms and stir into the mashed potato.

Grease the soufflé dishes and sprinkle an even layer of flour into them. Whip the egg white to a froth and stir this gently into the mashed potato. Divide the mixture among the soufflé dishes.

Cook over water in a 180°C oven for 18 mins.

For the sauce Cut the shallot into small cubes and fry them in butter. Add the mushrooms. When the mushrooms are cooked, pour in the cream and sour cream and allow to boil for a moment. Finally add the seasoning.

Smoked reindeer with baked turnip

To serve 4 persons

200 g cold or hot-smoked reindeer meat
4 small turnips
2 dl sour cream
1 dl whipping cream
salt and freshly ground white pepper
a little grated nutmeg
4 metal ring moulds 5–6 cm in diameter and about 3 cm high

Peel the turnips and cut them into thin, circular slices which will fit inside the ring moulds. Place pieces of kitchen foil under the moulds, grease them and arrange them on an oven tray.

Mix the sour cream and whipping cream and season with salt, white pepper and nutmeg.

Pour a little of the sour cream mixture into the bottom of each ring, then a slice of turnip, followed by more cream, and so on until the mould is full.

Bake in a 190° oven for about 25 mins. (Check that they are all properly done before taking them out of the oven.) Allow them to cool down for a moment, so that it will be easier to slip the moulds off.

Serve with very thin slices of smoked reindeer meat.

Life in the land of salt and allspice

IF ANYONE WERE TO ASK me why I decided to move to Finland, which was still regarded as a gastronomic backwater at that time, I would not know what to answer. Maybe it was just a young man's enthusiasm for new challenges that brought me here.

When my colleagues expressed surprise and curiosity, all I could do was answer with the modesty of a Finnish javelin thrower before the Olympic Games: "I'll just go and try my best – and see where it will get me!"

MODESTY WAS IN FACT the order of the day, for a young immigrant stepping into the kitchens of a Finnish restaurant in the early 1970s would inevitably be in for a fair dose of culture shock.

No one had any time for pure Finnish ingredients in those days. "Fine food" was prepared in the best restaurants using expensive imported raw materials and canned goods. Even a simple garnish such as boiled beetroot would be added to a stew straight out of an imported can. Salt and allspice were sprinkled liberally on more or less any food to add flavour, both in the kitchen and at the table, while herbs were rarely on offer. Fresh parsley and chives were things that only grew in country gardens.

I REMEMBER BEST being amazed at why the most common Finnish fish were seldom to be found on a restaurant menu, although many people would eat Baltic herring, perch or pike almost daily at home.

Fortunately, times are changing!

The mother of a new, more cheerful style of restaurant

WHO CAN SAY what the world of restaurants in Helsinki in the 1970s would have been like without Ragni Rissanen? For this young, foreign chef it would at least have been a very much more grim, monotonous place.

In the midst of a Finnish restaurant culture dominated by a number of big chains, Ragni was a delightful exception: a bold, independent-minded entrepreneur and pioneer for whom quality and style have always been more important than a few extra marks in profit. At the time when I was beginning my career in this land of salt and allspice, Ragni was still tending her fairly new chain of restaurants like a Karelian mother presiding over her huge family. She directed and trained her staff at the Rivoli in Albertinkatu, close to the old Opera House, and the Red Hat in Keskuskatu, in the heart of the city, almost like children of her own, and it would seem that on the side she managed to train a whole new generation of clients as well.

When I came to the Red Hat as head chef, Ragni's restaurants had been accepted by the people of Helsinki as places where you could find good food and a continental atmosphere.

FRENCH CUISINE had always been her great love, and I think she must have been the first restaurateur to fly fresh ingredients in directly from Paris – fish, shellfish, asparagus, artichokes etc. We in the kitchens were then sent to the airport to fetch them.

But Ragni was never satisfied only with imported foods and well-tried recipes. She was one of the first to be inspired by the nouvelle cuisine of France, and encouraged us to use the best local ingredients, according to the precepts of Michel Guérard and the other leaders of this movement. Ragni's kitchens were also ready to cross the boundaries of other gastronomic cultures without prejudice. One good example of this is the highly popular lunchtime "sweet & sauer" Baltic herrings from her Red Hat days, the recipe for which appears on the next page. The name as it appeared on the Finnish menu defied all language barriers, and the taste is a glorious mixture of cultures extending all the way from Sipoo to Shanghai!

RAGNI IS TO MY MIND an amusing blend of the traditional Finnish farmer's wife and the stylish "Madame" of a star-quality French restaurant who is equal to all eventualities. Ragni, if anyone, has always led by example. Whenever an extra pair of hands was needed in the kitchens, she was the first to be ready to grab an apron and roll up her sleeves. On the afternoon when we took the photograph of her for this book, she announced that she was going to her hotel early the following morning to help out in the kitchens at breakfast, as "assistant cook", as the Commercial Counsellor was happy enough to describe herself.

Would that every young man setting out on a career in catering could have a mentor and "surrogate mother" like her!

Ragni visiting the Helsinki Culinary Institute in summer 2004.

Sweet & sauer Baltic herrings

To serve 4 persons

24 whole Baltic herrings, cleaned
butter for frying
salt

For the sweet & sour sauce
   0.75 l water
   1.5 dl strong wine vinegar
   60 g sugar
   salt
   2 bay leaves
   10 whole black peppers
   8 juniper berries
   1 carrot
   1 small leek
   1 red onion
   chives for garnishing

Fry the herrings in butter until crisp. Allow to cool.

To prepare the sweet & sour sauce Bring the water to the boil in a saucepan with the wine vinegar, sugar and spices.

Wash the carrot and cut it and the leek into thin slices and the onion into shreds. Put the vegetables into the stock, allow them to cook for a moment and then put the stock on one side to cool.

Spread the fried herrings out on a shallow dish and pour the cooled sweet & sour sauce and vegetables on top of them.

Allow the dish to stand in the fridge overnight. Garnish with whole stems of chives and serve cold as a starter with boiled potatoes.

Mascarpone in my suitcase

ON THE TOP FLOOR was the Palace Gourmet, Finland's first restaurant to qualify for a star in the Michelin Guide, with Eero Mäkelä in charge of its kitchens, and lower down, on the second floor, was La Vista, thought of by many as the best Italian restaurant in town and the place where all the up-and-coming people in Helsinki society wanted to be seen.

All the pastas served at La Vista were "home-made", products of what must have been the first electric pasta maker in Finland.

WHEN I STARTED at La Vista in 1986 Finland still had a long way to go before joining the EU, so that the obtaining of genuine Italian ingredients was still subject to all manner of customs duties, import payments and restrictions.

One of the favourites on our menu was Tiramisu, which we prepared according to the original recipe – making us probably the first restaurant to do so in the whole city. Now, twenty years later, I dare to confess that we made our "genuine" Tiramisu with Finnish cottage cheese, as mascarpone was simply unobtainable. It was good, even so, although I wouldn't perhaps venture to call it tiramisu nowadays.

LATER, THROUGH THE FAR-SIGHTEDNESS of the management, we succeeded in establishing relations with a number of restaurants in Italy and were able to visit them regularly. Along with all our other paraphernalia, our baggage always included at least one extra, empty suitcase, which would usually be filled on the return journey with cheeses – mascarpone, provolone and mozzarella – and of course salami, ham and sun-dried tomatoes.

Gradually our "regulars" at the Palace began to remember us with little gifts when they came back from trips to Italy; in fact, one especially faithful customer marched into the kitchens one day with a whole Parma ham! As I know that he is also very fond of Finnish crayfish, I decided for the sake of old times to try an interesting combination of these with Italian pasta. It's surprising how well they go together!

Pasta and crayfish tails in Finlandia Vodka and cream sauce

For the pasta dough
- 300 g durum or plain wheat flour
- 3 eggs
- a little oil
- water as required

For the sauce
- about 10 boiled crayfish tails per person
- 3 dl whipping cream
- 8 cl Finlandia Vodka
- 1 small bunch of dill
- 1 shallot
- 30 g butter
- salt and freshly ground white pepper

Prepare the pasta dough, wrap it in cling foil and allow it to stand in the fridge for half an hour.

Roll the dough out into a thin sheet and cut it into ribbons in the manner of tagliatelle with a pasta maker (or pasta cutter).

Cook the pasta in a generous amount of water seasoned with sea salt for about 4 mins, until it is just al dente.

While the pasta is cooking, prepare the sauce.

Finely chop the shallot and fry it gently in the butter. Pour in the Finlandia Vodka and whipping cream and allow to boil for a moment. Finally add the dill, finely chopped.

Drop the crayfish tails into the sauce and season, but don't let the sauce boil any longer.

Pour the water off the pasta, add the sauce to the pasta and mix well. Serve at once.

Salmon and scallop carpaccio

To serve 4 persons

For the carpaccio
    a 400 g fillet of salmon
    flesh from 10 scallops
    20 basil leaves
    freshly ground sea salt and white pepper
    cling foil

For the dressing
    1 dl pale olive oil
    2 tbsp lemon juice
    salt and freshly ground black pepper

To prepare the carpaccio Remove the skin from the salmon and pick out any remaining bones with pincers.

Place the fillet on a chopping board with its outer side facing down and cut a slice lengthways from its thick centre part, beginning at the "backbone". Don't cut this slice away from the fillet entirely but leave it partly attached. Turn the slice outwards like the cover of a book. Now you will have a broad fillet of even thickness which it will be easy to roll.

Season the salmon with freshly ground sea salt and white pepper, spread a sheet of cling foil on the working surface and place the fillet onto it.

Cut the scallops into slices about 3 mm thick, spread these evenly on top of the salmon and cover with basil leaves.

Roll the salmon fillet up tightly with the help of the cling foil in the manner of a traditional swiss roll, starting from the tail and working towards the head. Finally straighten the foil by pulling on both ends at once and close the ends of the roll.

Put the roll into a freezer until it is frozen right through and can easily be cut into very thin slices with a sharp knife.

To prepare the dressing Shake the salt and pepper into the lemon juice, add the oil and mix well.

When the salmon roll is sufficiently well frozen, take it out of the freezer, remove the foil and cut the roll into the thinnest possible slices. Arrange these on a plate and brush them with dressing. Garnish with basil leaves.

Finnish strawberries Italian style

To serve 4 persons

250 g strawberries
200 g ricotta cheese
1 dl whipping cream
fresh spinach leaves
fresh basil leaves
a little sugar
salt and black pepper
balsámico vinegar

Whip the cream and mix with the ricotta cheese, add a generous amount of chopped basil and season with salt and pepper.

Arrange the spinach and basil leaves on a plate and spoon out the ricotta mixture on top of them. Make an attractive mound of strawberries in the centre and sprinkle them with a little balsámico and caster sugar

Ville de Paris and his salmon soup

I MUST HAVE KNOWN about Ville Vallgren's salmon soup long before I had any idea of who this outstanding figure of Finnish sculpture, renowned gourmet and connoisseur of the art of good living actually was – in spite of having passed by his most famous work, the Havis Amanda statue more or less daily on my way to the Market Place or the Old Market Hall in Helsinki. In fact this same statue has kept cropping up on my way to work since then – whether I have been going to the Palace Hotel, the Savoy or Kanavaranta.

I don't know for sure where the idea first arose to start making this soup according to the original recipe; it may have been at the König Restaurant or at the Savoy, but we used to make it quite often with Eero at the Kanavaranta, and always with great success.

Once the connection between the soup and the sculpture dawned on me, I started to look a little further into the achievements of this cultural figure.

VALLGREN, or "Ville de Paris", as his fellow artists used to call him, lived and worked in Paris up to 1913, and it was there that he acquired his jovial interest in gastronomy and wines and developed these things practically into an art. It was there, too, that the Sirach Fraternity came into being, a company of connoisseurs of wine made up mostly of artists, as the founder members included Albert Edelfelt and the celebrated Swedish painters Carl Larsson and Ernst Josephson. The fraternity continued to function after Vallgren's return to Finland, and many notable Finnish artistic and literary figures, from Akseli Gallen-Kallela to Eino Leino, belonged to it.

Following his nomination to a professorship, Vallgren lived at his studio home of Villa Paarmio at Leppävaara in Espoo from 1913 onwards. There his daily routine consisted of sculpturing and extensive culinary exploits of a kind that modern-day gastronomes can only dream about. Books were even published about them, including *Mat och dryck med roliga gubbar* (1917) and *Wille-Gubbens Matkatekes* (1921).

I BEGAN TO FEEL a great deal of empathy with Vallgren once I realized that he was a great admirer of Finnish fish, in spite of his famed penchant for lutfisk at Christmas, accompanied by a good Mosel white wine!

Ville Vallgren's Little Catechism of Food contains many valuable thoughts on life and our daily bread. His sixth commandment, for instance, reads:

"If you love your neighbour as yourself, you will grant him just as good food and drink as you would wish to enjoy yourself."

Ville Vallgren's salmon soup

400 g of salmon fillet cut into thumb-sized cubes
4 large onions thinly sliced (about 400 g)
2 salted or pickled cucumbers
100 g fresh champignons, sliced
1 tbsp capers
8 stoneless black olives
12 stoneless green olives
50 g tomato purée
1.5 l fish stock
50 g butter
1 tbsp flour

For the bouquet garni
1 bay leaf
1 sprig of thyme
6 whole white peppers and 6 whole allspice
1 clove of garlic, crushed
coarse sea salt

Cut the onions in half and slice them thinly.

Melt the butter in a saucepan, add the slices of onion and allow to simmer over a gentle heat for about 15 mins, stirring constantly. Add the tomato purée and simmer for another 5 mins. Add the flour and allow it to soak up the liquid.

Heat the fish stock and pour it into the saucepan alternately with the onion and tomato purée.

Put the bouquet garni into the saucepan and allow the whole mixture to boil gently for about 45 mins.

Peel the cucumbers and cut them into four lengthways and then into small triangles. Add these with the champignons, capers and whole olives to the mixture and allow to boil gently for another 10 mins. Take out the bouquet garni.

Finally add the cubes of salmon and boil for just a moment, as they will cook very quickly. Add fish stock as necessary, remembering that the soup is intended to be fairly thick.

Summer cucumber soup

To serve 4 persons

1 fresh cucumber
1 tsp salt
1 clove of garlic
juice of 1 lemon
crushed white pepper
1/4 tsp caraway seed
8 dl plain yoghurt
1 bunch of chervil

Peel the cucumber, cut it in half down the centre and remove the seeds with a spoon. Cut it into pieces and put them in a liquidizer.

Add the clove of garlic, peeled, the salt, lemon juice, white pepper, caraway seed and chervil. Turn the liquidizer on and pour in the yoghurt. Mix well and check for taste.

Allow the soup to stand in the cool for some time before serving.

Beetroot and basil soup

To serve 4 persons

400 g fresh beetroots
50 g butter
1 l vegetable stock
a bunch of fresh basil
nutmeg
salt and white pepper
1 dl sour cream

Peel the beetroots and cut them up into small pieces. Allow them to simmer in butter first and then add the vegetable stock and allow them to boil until cooked.

Add the chopped basil and blend to a purée. Season with nutmeg, salt and pepper. Finally add the sour cream.

Sweet pepper and tomato soup with goat's cheese

To serve 4 persons

4 large sweet peppers
8 large tomatoes
1 dl olive oil
20 g fructose
8 dl vegetable stock
salt and white pepper
1.5 dl whipped cream
80 g soft goat's cheese

Cut the sweet peppers and tomatoes in half to remove the seeds and then cut them into cubes.

Pour the oil into a warm saucepan, add the peppers and allow to cook.

Add the tomatoes and fructose, boil for a moment and then add the vegetable stock. Cook gently until the peppers and tomatoes are soft. Reduce to a soup in a liquidizer and season with salt and pepper.

Return the soup to the saucepan and add the whipped cream. Serve out and place a small round of goat's cheese neatly on top of each portion.

Boletus soup

To serve 4 persons

400 g fresh mushrooms, preferably Boletus edulis
1 onion
50 g butter
10 g parsley stalks, chopped
4 tbsp flour
2 l good meat stock
12 cl sherry
1.5 dl whipped cream
salt and freshly ground white pepper
a handful of dried Boletus edulis for garnishing

Cut the mushrooms into fingertip-sized pieces. Chop the onion and parsley stalks. Heat the butter in a saucepan and sauté the onion. Add the mushrooms and parsley, stir and cook lightly for a moment more. Sprinkle flour on the mushrooms and mix well. Then pour the stock over the mushrooms, stirring constantly. When the mixture has returned to the boil, add the seasoning, checking the taste of the stock before adding any more salt.

When the contents of the saucepan have boiled for 15–20 mins, pour them into a liquidizer and reduce to a soup.

Return the soup to the saucepan and heat if necessary. Finally add the sherry and whipped cream.

Serve out and garnish each portion with crushed dried mushrooms.

I don't usually recommend wine with the soup course, but in this case a glass of dry fino sherry is more or less a must.

Gero's sauerkraut soup

To make 6 portions

1 leek
60 g butter
150 g raw potatoes, diced
450 g sauerkraut
1 l good meat stock
3 tbsp sherry vinegar
2.5 dl cream
1/2 tsp ground caraway seed
2 bay leaves
5 juniper berries
salt, pepper

Wash the leek well and cut it into small strips. Cook these in butter in a thick-bottomed saucepan. Be careful not to brown them!

Add the potatoes, sauerkraut, bay leaves and juniper berries and allow to simmer for about 3 mins.

Pour in the stock and vinegar and boil for about 20 mins.

Add the cream and return the mixture to the boil for a moment. Take out the bay leaves and juniper berries.

Pour into a liquidizer, reduce to a soup and sieve. Serve on heated plates.

Pork sausage soup flavoured with saffron

To serve 6 persons

300 g Finnish pork sausages (siskonmakkara)
1.2 l vegetable stock
40 g thin strips of leek
60 g diced carrot
2 potatoes, diced
40 g diced turnip
40 g chopped cauliflower
40 g chopped celeriac
40 g diced marrow
2 knife-tips saffron
1 bay leaf
2 tbsp finely chopped parsley

Heat up the stock, add the saffron, bay leaf and all the diced and chopped vegetables. Cook over a gentle heat.

Pass the sausages between the forefinger and middle finger and form them into small, fingertip-sized pieces. Cook them in the stock. Check the taste.

Add the parsley before serving.

SIMPLY DELICIOUS!

Pike *(Esox lucius)*   Pike-perch *(Lucioperca lucioperca)*

Perch *(Perca fluviatilis)*   Flounder *(Pleuronectes flesus)*

Spring pike in cucumber and mustard sauce

To serve 4 persons

4 smallish fillets of pike
1 fresh cucumber
1 bunch of dill
2 tbsp Dijon mustard
4 dl whipping cream
butter to grease the dish
salt and freshly ground white pepper

Peel the cucumber, remove the seeds and cut it into thin slices.

Mix the cream, mustard, salt and pepper together. Grease a baking dish, place the fish in it and spread the slices of cucumber and the chopped dill on top. Pour the cream over these and bake in a 185°C oven for about 15 mins.

Summer whitefish with butter sauce

To serve 4 persons

4 fillets of whitefish
mange-tout peas
cauliflower
tomatoes
a marrow
green asparagus
100 g whitefish roe
a few sprigs of dill

For the sauce

140 g unsalted butter in 1 x 1 cm cubes
1 finely chopped shallot
1 dl dry white wine
a drop of lemon juice
salt and freshly ground white pepper

Peel the asparagus and cut into pieces the size of your little finger. Cut the marrow open, remove the seeds and slice. Cut up the cauliflower. Scald the tomatoes, take out the seeds and cut into pieces.

Cook all the vegetables except for the tomatoes separately al dente and cool them in cold water.

Place the fish on a greased oven tray, skin upwards, make a few cuts across their skin with a sharp knife and season with sea salt.

Cook in a 250°C oven for about 6 mins.

To prepare the sauce Boil the chopped shallot in the wine in a saucepan until there is only a little liquid left. Stir in the cold cubes of butter gently one by one and then pass the sauce through a sieve. Season with lemon juice, salt and white pepper.

Finally heat the vegetables and pieces of tomato in a small amount of butter in a saucepan and season to taste.

Place the vegetables on a plate and the whitefish fillets on top of them. Pour the sauce round them and garnish with a sprig of dill and a teaspoonful of whitefish roe.

Whitefish cooked whole in foil

1 scaled whitefish
50 g butter
a small bunch of dill
salt and freshly ground white pepper
a sheet of aluminium foil

Grease the foil, which should be about ten centimetres longer than the fish. Place the fish on the foil, with the rest of the butter and the dill in its stomach and season with salt and pepper.

Close the package tightly and bake in a 220°C oven for about 25 mins.

Smoked fillet of whitefish with butter sauce and new potatoes

To serve 4 persons

4 whitefish fillets weighing about 150 g each
finely ground salt
a smoking box
1 dl alder chippings

For the butter sauce
stems of 4 spring onions
0.5 dl fish stock
0.5 dl dry white wine
100 g unsalted butter
salt and pepper from a mill as required

Lightly grease the grid of the smoking box and place the fish on it.

Spread the alder chippings evenly on the bottom of the box and place the grid into it. Close the lid of the box and put it onto an open fire or a barbeque grill.

Smoke the fish for about 8 mins, then lift the lid carefully and check whether the fish is cooked.

If it is not yet entirely cooked, close the lid and leave the box to stand for a moment.

For the butter sauce Wash the onion stems and cut them into small pieces.

Cut the cold butter into cubes of about 1x1 cm and put them back in the fridge.

Pour the fish stock and white wine into a pan and boil until about half the liquid is left.

Take the cubes of butter from the fridge and stir them into the hot stock 2 or 3 at a time. Don't let the sauce boil.

Finally add the chopped onion stems and serve with the warm fish and boiled new potatoes.

Fillets of perch with mushroom, sweetbread and crayfish stuffing

To serve 4 persons

8 medium-sized fillets of perch
salt
100 g butter

For the stuffing
100 g finely chopped, thoroughly blanched false morels (Gyromitra esculenta)
150 g well-cooked sweetbreads
1 tbsp chopped leek
30 g butter
2 dl whipping cream
salt and freshly ground white pepper
chopped dill
50 g peeled crayfish tails or prawns

Carefully bone the perch fillets (see instructions on p. 63). Season with salt and fry quickly in butter. Keep warm. Handle the fillets with care so that they will not break into pieces.

To prepare the stuffing Boil the mushrooms in at least two changes of water to ensure that the toxin has been removed (for more precise instructions on how to handle this poisonous mushroom, see p. 134).

Fry them lightly in butter together with the sweetbreads, cut into small pieces, and the chopped leek. Add the cream and bring to the boil until the mixture has thickened. Season with salt and pepper and add the dill. Mix the crayfish tails or prawns into the stuffing just before serving, so that they do not cook and become leathery.

Place a perch fillet on each plate with its inner surface facing upwards, spread hot stuffing on it and cover with another fillet, with its outer surface facing upwards. Garnish with dill and serve with boiled potatoes and vegetables according to season.

Perch steaks filled with spinach

To serve 4 persons

8 fillets of perch
300 g blanched spinach
1 shallot
1 clove of garlic
80 g butter

Cut the shallot and clove of garlic into small pieces and fry them lightly in butter.

Add the blanched spinach and stir to make sure that the ingredients are well mixed. Season with salt, freshly ground white pepper and a sprinkling of nutmeg.

Bone the perch fillets (see instructions on p. 63) and fry them in butter. Season with salt and white pepper to taste.

Place one fillet on each plate, spread the spinach mixture on it and cover with another fillet. Serve with boiled potatoes.

SIMPLY DELICIOUS!

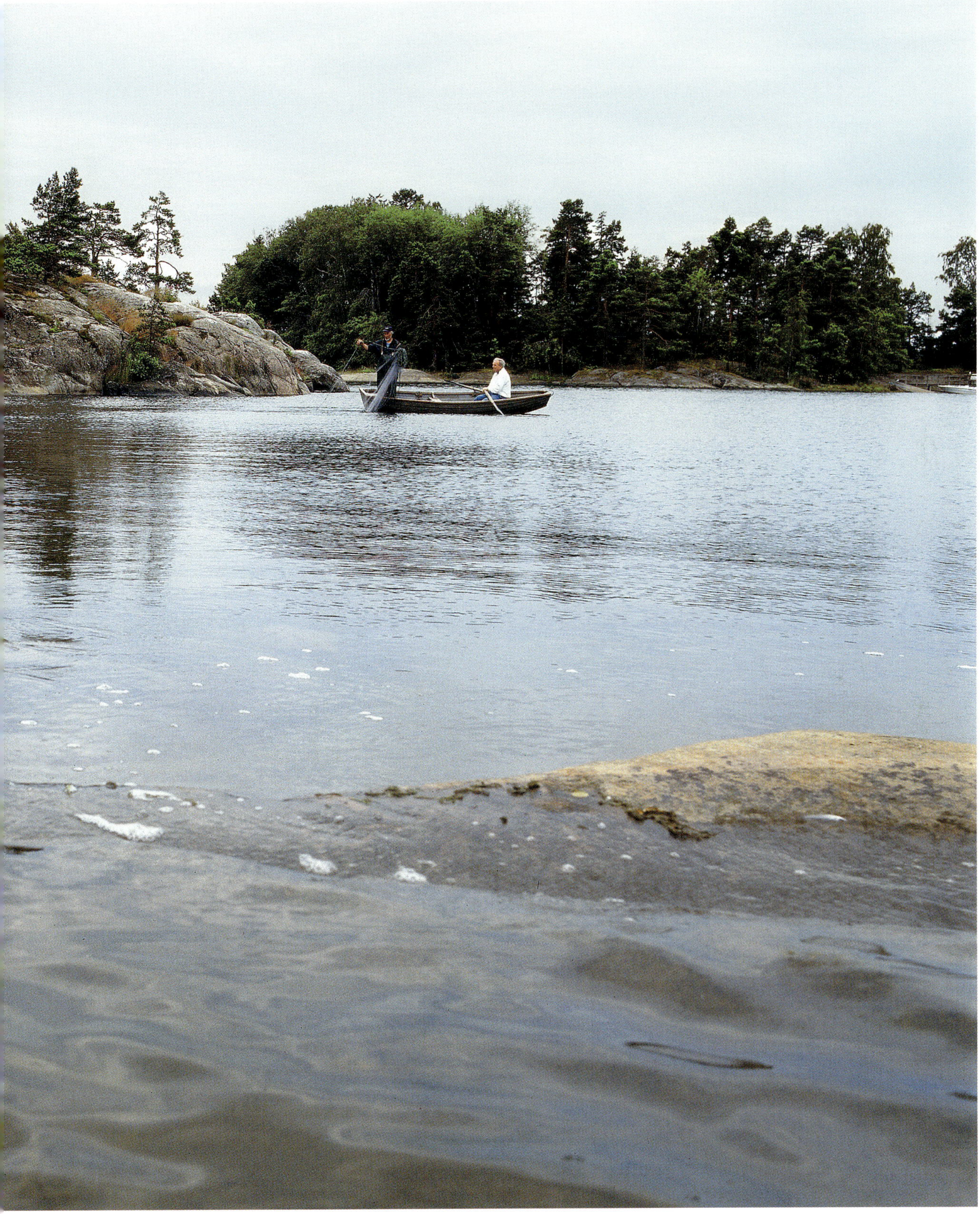

Three-fish selyanka in the Marski style.

The Russian thickened fish soup known as *selyanka* (see p. 135) was one of the favourite dishes of the Finnish military commander, president and noted gourmet Field-Marshal C. G. E. Mannerheim, or "Marski". Thereby hangs a tale of dubious origin.

It is said that when he was served selyanka made of three fish species, salmon, pike-perch and perch, for the first time at the Savoy Restaurant he was rather put off by it, as he believed that one should not mix basic ingredients in that way.

The whole story may be pure fiction, however, as he had grown enormously fond of selyanka during the time when he served in the Imperial Chevalier Guards in St. Petersburg and had sent the recipe to his sister, Eva Mannerheim-Sparre, who published it in her famous cookery book.

As far as the three-fish version of the soup is concerned, all we know is that he enjoyed it innumerable times at the Savoy.

The Marshal of Finland and a German chef – at the same restaurant, but at different times

IT MUST HAVE BEEN FATE that brought me to restaurants called the Savoy. I began in one as a piccolo 27 years ago, and in 1991 I found myself in another, one of Finland's most prestigious and traditional restaurants.

The formal opening of the Savoy Restaurant in Helsinki took place on 3rd June 1937, attended by a distinguished group of invited guests, as the saying goes. Field-Marshal Mannerheim was not present on that occasion as he was celebrating his 70th birthday the very next day, but he lunched there a couple of days later and was to enjoy innumerable lunches and dinners at the Savoy in the following years.

Tradition has it that on his very first visit he chose a table that was to his liking in a peaceful corner close to the door to the kitchens and that he always asked for the same table from that time on. The result was that "Marski's table" became so famous and popular that it was always booked up for weeks in advance.
I even remember cases of clients cancelling their whole lunch or dinner reservation because they couldn't sit at Marski's table.

But those who did get a booking there almost always ordered his other well-known favourite, *vorschmack* (see p. 135).

TO MARK THE 125TH ANNIVERSARY of Field-Marshal Mannerheim's birth in 1992, we decided to arrange a week of celebrations featuring his favourite foods. We designed two luncheon menus to offer during the week and a long formal dinner menu to be served on his actual birthday, June 4th.

The dinner began, of course, with vorschmack, followed by pâté de fois gras, three-fish selyanka, fillet of lamb and apple tart. The main course of one of the lunch menus was fried pike-perch Mannerheim-style.

THERE ARE HUNDREDS OF TALES in circulation about the Field-Marshal's gastronomic preferences, with innumerable variants on each. One of these is connected with the pike-perch, or zander.

One old and utterly reliable source tells us that Mannerheim's fillet of pike-perch was served with horseradish butter and a thick sauce of chopped champignons, while a still older and still more reliable source maintains that the same pike-perch was definitely always served just with horseradish butter. I wouldn't know, but on our anniversary menu it came without the mushroom sauce, and I have often prepared it in that way since.

This famous pike-perch, by the way, is excellent for serving to visitors at home, as it is quick and easy to prepare even for a large number of people. It will always succeed if you start out with good, fresh fish – and it will taste simply delicious!

Fried pike-perch Mannerheim-style

To serve 4 persons

4 skinless fillets of pike-perch
flour
breadcrumbs
salt
butter
4 tbsp freshly grated horseradish
melted butter

Bone the fillets (see instructions on p. 63).

Cover them on both sides with flour and breadcrumbs and cook in butter in a frying pan. When done, take them out of the pan onto the plates and keep warm.

Add more melted butter to the pan and fry the grated horseradish in it very lightly, taking care not to let it burn.

Pour this horseradish butter over the pike-perch fillets and serve with boiled potatoes and steamed vegetables according to season.

Pike-perch oriental style

To serve 4 persons

4 fillets of pike-perch
sea salt from a mill
1 small marrow
400 g shitake mushrooms
1 small leek
1 clove of garlic
3 tbsp cooking oil
1 dl soy sauce
2 dl white wine
2 sprigs of fresh coriander
salt and freshly ground white pepper
a drop of sherry

Split the marrow lengthways, spoon out the seeds and cut it crossways into slices 1 cm thick. Slice the mushrooms, leek and clove of garlic as well.

Heat the oil in a wok, lightly fry the leek and garlic, and then add the marrow and mushroom slices. Cook al dente.

Add the soy sauce and white wine and allow to boil for a moment. Finally add the coriander. Season with white pepper, sherry and salt to taste.

Place the fish fillets on a greased oven tray, skin side upwards, and season with sea salt.

Heat the oven's grill or upper element to 285°C and place the fish in the top of the oven to toast for about 4 mins.

Fried fillet of pike-perch, ratatouille and rosemary sauce

To serve 4 persons

4 fillets of pike-perch
50 g butter for frying
sea salt

For the ratatouille
2 carrots
1 cauliflower
2 turnips
100 g French beans
2 tomatoes
1 tbsp finely chopped parsley
butter
salt and freshly ground white pepper

For the rosemary sauce
1 shallot
1 dl white wine
4 cl Noilly Prat vermouth
2 dl fish stock
3 sprigs of fresh rosemary
1.5 dl whipping cream
salt and white pepper

Remove the remaining bones from the fillets (see instructions on p. 63), season and fry in butter just before serving.

To prepare the ratatouille Peel the carrots and turnips and cut them into small cubes. Cut the cauliflower into florets about the size of the top of your thumb. Top and tail the beans and cut them into small pieces. Cook all the vegetables separately al dente.

Scald the tomatoes, take out the seeds and cut into cubes.

Melt the butter in a saucepan, pour onto the cooked vegetables and season with salt and pepper. Finally add the diced tomatoes and finely chopped parsley.

To prepare the rosemary sauce Peel the shallot and cut it into small cubes. Pour the white wine and vermouth into a saucepan and add the pieces of shallot. Boil until most of the liquid has evaporated and then add the fish stock and sprigs of rosemary and boil again until about half of the liquid is left. Pour in the cream, season and allow the sauce to boil until thick. Then sieve it and keep it warm.

Spread a pool of sauce on the plate, arrange a neat pile of ratatouille on it and place a fried fillet of pike-perch on the top. Garnish with a sprig of rosemary.

Pike-perch Mediterranean style

1 whole pike-perch, scaled
1 orange
2 tomatoes
1 marrow
10 green olives
1 bay leaf
3 dl dry white wine
salt and fresh ground white pepper
butter to grease the dish

Grease an oven dish.

Peel the orange and cut it into pieces. Cut the tomatoes in half, spoon out the seeds and cut the remainder into strips. Cut the marrow lengthways, remove the seeds and slice crossways.

Season the fish inside and out with salt and white pepper. Place it in the dish and add the other ingredients. Pour the white wine on top and cook in a 185°C oven for about 20 mins.

Fried flounder with dill and crayfish filling

To serve 4 persons

4 large flounders
butter for frying
250 g crayfish tails, cooked and peeled
a small bunch of dill
0.5 dl fish stock
150 g unsalted butter
1 tsp lemon juice
salt and freshly ground white pepper

Clean the flounders, rinse them well and fold them into pockets to hold the filling by first opening them up down the backbone on the dark-coloured side and then partly cutting the fillets loose on both sides of the backbone.

Season the fish with salt and pepper and fry them fairly well in butter on both sides. Lift them out onto an oven tray.

Melt about 20 g of butter in a saucepan. Heat the crayfish tails well in this but do not cook them, or they will become tough.

Turn the warm crayfish tails and their liquid out into another saucepan, add the fish stock and bring to the boil. Then whip in the rest of the butter in small cubes, add the lemon juice and season with salt and pepper. Finally stir in the finely chopped dill.

Bake the fish in a 200°C oven for about 4 mins. Lift them out onto plates, fill the "pockets" with the crayfish tails and pour a little of the sauce onto them and the remainder around them. Serve with boiled potatoes and vegetables according to season.

Quick salmon quenelles in champagne sauce

To serve 4 persons

For the salmon quenelles
   300 g salmon
   1 egg whipping cream
   grated nutmeg
   salt and freshly ground white pepper
   1 dl fish stock for cooking them

For the champagne sauce
   30 g butter
   3 tbsp flour
   3 dl fish stock
   3 dl dry champagne or sparkling wine
   salt and freshly ground white pepper
   1 dl whipped cream

To prepare the salmon quenelles Cut the salmon into pieces about 3 x 3 cm and return them to the fridge for a moment.

After they have cooled again, crush them in a liquidizer, gradually adding ice-cold whipped cream and the white of an egg. Season with nutmeg, salt and pepper and put the bowl back into the fridge to cool.

Grease a deep oven dish, shape the fish mixture into neat cakes with two tablespoons, put them into the dish and pour 1 dl fish stock on them. Cover the dish with aluminium foil and cook in a 200°C oven for about 20 mins.

To prepare the champagne sauce Melt the butter in a saucepan, add the flour and stir well. Pour in the heated fish stock in two parts, stirring well all the time. Then add the champagne or sparkling wine and allow to boil for a moment. Season with salt and pepper. Finally, carefully add the whipped cream.

Serve with new potatoes and vegetables according to season.

A fish needs its bones for swimming in the water, but not on your plate! A simple way to take all the bones out of a fillet of perch or pike-perch is to run your finger lightly along the inner surface of the fillet from head to tail. You will be able to feel very easily whether there are any small, sharp bones left. Take a very sharp knife and make an inward-slanting cut down to the skin on either side of the mid-line. If you now cut out the sharp triangle formed in this way, the rest of the bones will come with it.

False morel and salmon sandwich with hollandaise sauce

To serve 4 persons

8 thin slices of salmon
1 finely chopped onion
300 g well-blanched false morels (Gyromitra esculenta)
a little dill
50 g butter
salt and pepper

For the hollandaise sauce

5 egg yolks
300 g melted unsalted butter
1 dl water
salt and freshly ground white pepper
1 tbsp freshly squeezed lemon juice

Arrange the slices of salmon on a greased oven tray. Heat the grill or upper element of the oven to 285°C.

Fry the chopped onion in butter in a frying pan, add the mushrooms (for instructions on handling these poisonous mushrooms, see p. 134), season with salt and pepper and finally add the finely chopped dill.

Now make the hollandaise sauce.

Bring the water to the boil with some salt and freshly ground white pepper in it, allow to cool, add the egg yolks and whisk over a hot but not boiling water bath until the mixture thickens.

Whisk the butter in gradually, one knob at a time. Season with lemon juice. Sieve the sauce through a muslin cloth if necessary.

Cook the slices of salmon in the oven for about 2 mins.

Put one slice on each plate first, spread the mushroom mixture on it and cover with another slice.

Pour hollandaise sauce over the sandwiches – and revel in the taste of early summer in Finland!

Salmon, kohlrabi and basil froth

To serve 4 persons

4 pieces of salmon fillet, 150 g/person
1–2 kohlrabi
salt

For the basil froth
    1 dl dry white wine
    1 tbsp dry vermouth
    1 shallot
    5 dl fish stock
    1 bunch of basil
    150 g unsalted butter

Peel the kohlrabi and cut into discs just over 1 cm thick. Cut these into sticks about 0.5 cm wide and reduce them to macaroni-like strips with a cheese slicer or asparagus knife. (The strips in the picture have been produced using a machine, which can be found in most well-stocked kitchen appliance shops.)

Cook these "macaroni" strips al dente in boiling salt water and rinse them quickly in cold water.

To prepare the basil froth Finely chop the shallot, put it into a saucepan with the white wine and vermouth and bring to the boil. Add the fish stock and the stems of the basil. Allow to boil until a third of the original volume is left.

Sieve the stock and add the basil leaves, cut into strips. Pour the stock into a liquidizer, turn the machine on and add small knobs of butter one by one. Season with salt if necessary.

Fry the pieces of salmon quickly in a hot pan, first on the skin side and then on both sides, then place them on an oven tray and bake them at 200°C for 6 mins.

Steam the kohlrabi strips quickly on the bottom of a saucepan, pour the basil froth over them and mix. Make a neat pile of this mixture in the centre of the plate and place a piece of salmon on top.

Tomato and ginger herrings

To serve 4 persons

800 g filleted Baltic herrings
1 shallot
1 tbsp grated fresh ginger
2 large scalded tomatoes
6 dl prepared tomato juice
salt and freshly ground pepper

Roll the herrings up with their skin on the outside. Grease an oven dish and arrange the herrings in it.

Peel and dice the shallot to form small cubes and mix with the tomato juice and ginger. Season with salt and pepper.

Cut the scalded tomatoes in half, remove the insides and cut the remainder into small cubes. Spread these on top of the herrings and then pour the tomato juice mixture into the dish.

Cover the dish with aluminium foil and cook in a 220°C oven for about 20 mins.

Serve warm with boiled or mashed potatoes. These herring rolls are also delicious cold as a starter.

Casseroled vendace

To serve 4 persons

700 g cleaned vendace (Coregonus albula)
2 shallots
1 leek
butter
salt and freshly ground white pepper
100 g bacon
3 tbsp finely chopped dill
8 dl fish stock
1 dl dry white wine

Chop the shallots, divide the leek down the centre and cut into strips.

Grease an oven dish and arrange the vendace in it with their heads all pointing in the same direction. Season with salt and pepper.

Cut the bacon into thin strips and fry in a pan until the fat in them has melted. Then scatter the pieces of bacon, shallot, leek and dill onto the vendace. Finally pour the fish stock and white wine over them.

Bake in a 200°C oven for about 18 mins.

Serve with boiled potatoes and dark rye bread.

Vendace deep fried in a beer dough

To serve 4 persons

600 g cleaned vendace
salt and white pepper
flour

For the dough
2 dl lager beer
2 dl flour
1 egg yolk
2 egg whites
salt
1 l rapeseed oil for frying

Mix the beer, flour and egg yolk together. Whip the egg whites into a froth and fold into the dough. Season with salt.

Season the vendace with salt and white pepper, flour them and cover them in dough, about 5 or 6 at a time.

Heat the oil to about 175°C in a large saucepan and drop the vendace in one by one.

When the fish are cooked and a golden brown colour on the outside, lift them out with a skimming ladle onto a dish covered with kitchen paper to drain.

Serve with good mashed potatoes.

Fillet of burbot with lemon-grass sauce

To serve 4 persons

600 g fillets of burbot (Lota lota)
1 chopped onion
1 bay leaf
coarse sea salt

For the sauce

2 stems of lemon-grass
1 small shallot
50 g butter
40 g flour
1 dl dry white wine
juice of half a lime
0.5 l fish stock
0.5 dl whipped cream
salt and freshly ground white pepper
200 g mange-tout peas
1 cauliflower
2 carrots

Begin by preparing the sauce.

Melt the butter in a saucepan, fry the lemon-grass in it in small pieces, and also the chopped onion. Pour in the white wine, lime juice and fish stock. Allow to simmer for about 15 mins, season with salt and freshly ground white pepper, sieve and add the whipped cream just before serving.

Cut the burbot fillets into pieces about 4 cm long and cook them in water seasoned with salt, the onion and the bay leaf.

Clean the mange-tout peas and cut up the carrots and cauliflower. Cook them al dente in salted water and serve with the fish and sauce.

SIMPLY DELICIOUS!

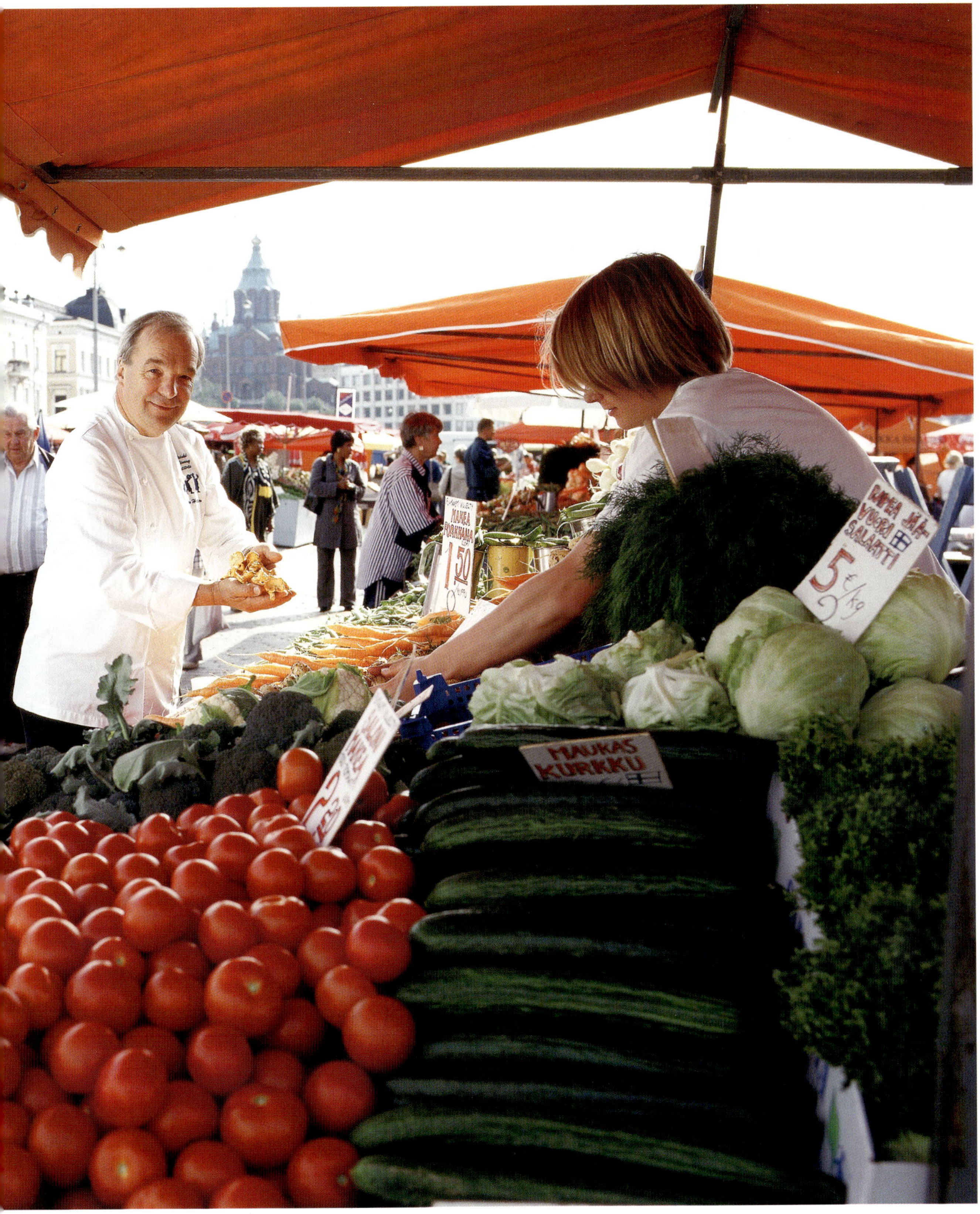
MAKEA PORKKANA
1,50
MAUKAS KURKKU
5 €/kg

Spinach cakes with watercress sauce

To serve 4 persons

600 g blanched fresh spinach
0.5 dl olive oil
2 small shallots
1 clove of garlic
2 tbsp stone pine seeds
grated nutmeg
salt and freshly ground pepper

For the watercress sauce

3 dl crème fraîche
6 tbsp watercress leaves
1/2 tsp sweet mustard
salt and freshly ground white pepper

Cut the blanched spinach into pieces with a kitchen knife and squeeze out the excess liquid. Cut the shallots and clove of garlic into small cubes.

Sauté the shallots and garlic in oil in a shallow saucepan or frying pan. Add the spinach and cook for a moment. Mix in the stone pine seeds and season with nutmeg, salt and pepper.

Form the spinach into firm, round cakes with a circular metal mould.

To prepare the sauce Put all the ingredients in a blender and switch on for about a minute. Pour into a bowl and season.

Serve the spinach cakes out onto plates and pour sauce around them.

Chanterelle and spring cabbage rolls

To serve 4 persons

a whole small spring cabbage
800 g chanterelles
a large onion
3 tomatoes
50 g butter
1 tbsp finely chopped parsley
1 tbsp finely chopped chervil
salt and white pepper from a mill

Carefully strip off eight good-looking leaves from the cabbage and cook them al dente in water. Pour off the water and allow the leaves to cool.

Chop the chanterelles into small pieces. Peel the onion and cut it up finely. Scald the tomatoes, take out the seeds and cut the remaining parts into small cubes.

Fry the onions lightly in butter in a frying pan and add the chanterelles. When these are cooked, add the cubes of tomato and the finely chopped herbs. Season with salt and pepper.

Lay the cabbage leaves out on a chopping board, spread the chanterelle mixture on them and roll them up neatly. Place the rolls in a greased oven dish and bake at 200°C for about 6 mins.

Serve the rolls with a red wine sauce (see p. 91) or madeira sauce (see p. 104).

Apple rings coated with sesame seeds and served with honey sauce

To serve 4 persons

For the apple rings

8 slices of apple about 1 cm thick
1 egg
1 dl flour
100 g sesame seeds
salt and white pepper
rapeseed oil for frying

For the honey sauce

2 tomatoes
8 radishes
1 bunch of chives
1 tsp finely chopped coriander leaves
2 dl plain yoghurt
1 dl whipping cream
2 tbsp liquid honey
salt and freshly ground white pepper

To prepare the apple rings Peel and core the apples and cut them into rings about 1 cm thick.

Rub first in flour, then in lightly whisked egg yolk and lastly in sesame seeds.

Fry them gently in rapeseed oil until they are a golden brown. Season them with salt and pepper.

To prepare the honey sauce Scald the tomatoes, cut them in half and remove the seeds, then cut them into even-sized cubes.

Grate the radishes into a bowl, add the chopped coriander leaves and finely chopped chives. Mix all these ingredients together and add the yoghurt and cream. Finally add the honey and season with salt and pepper.

Place a pool of sauce on the plate and arrange the apple rings on top.

Something green

SIMPLY DELICIOUS!

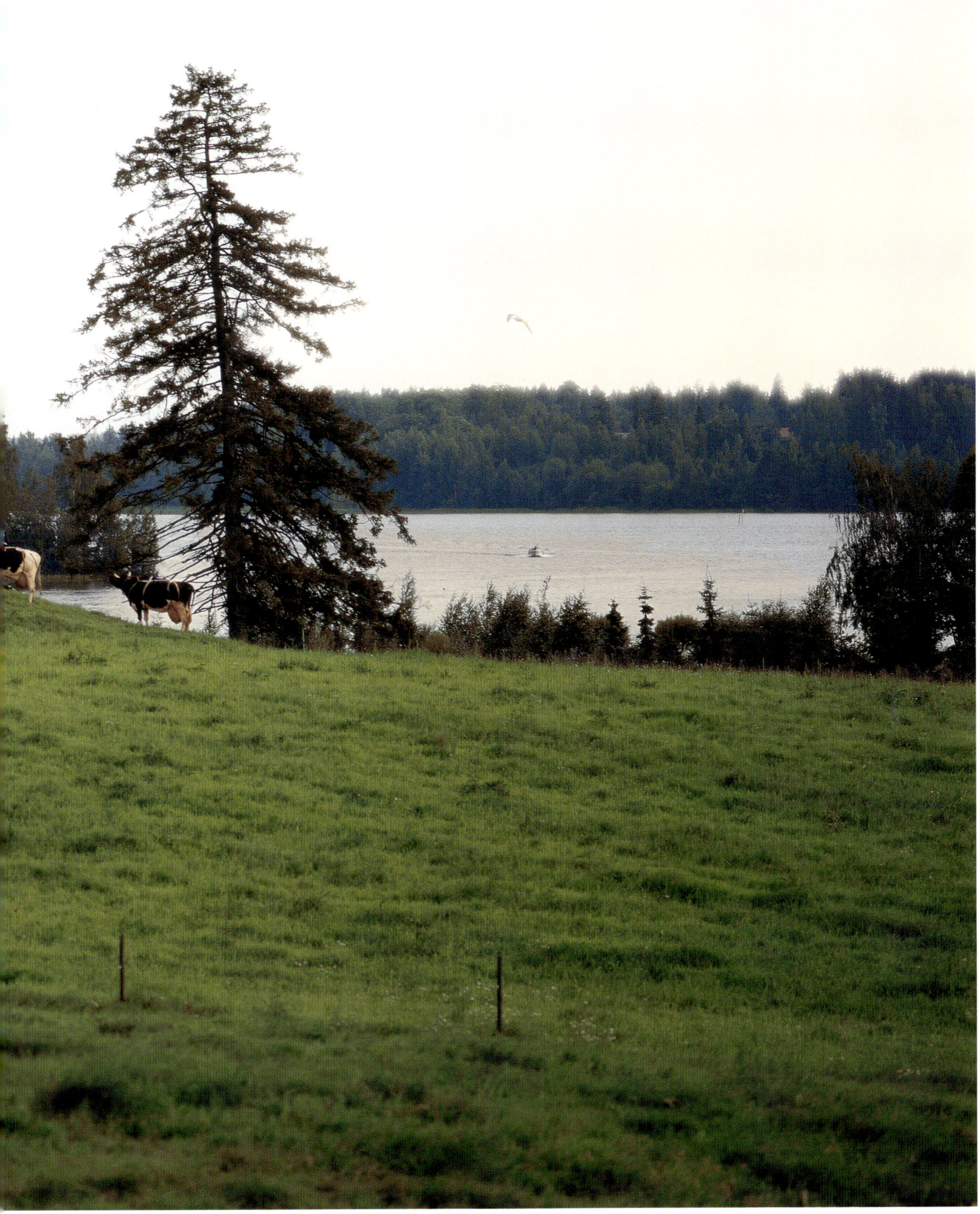

Entrecôte steaks with stone pine seeds and pistachios

To serve 4 persons

4 entrecôte steaks, about 150 g each
150 g stone pine seeds
100 g pistachio nuts
10 g fructose
8 juniper berries
100 g butter
2 tbsp finely chopped parsley
2 tsp Dijon mustard
salt and freshly ground black pepper
4 small tomatoes
1 endive
salt and freshly ground pepper

Roast the pine seeds and pistachios in a frying pan with the fructose and grind them together with the juniper seeds in a blender.

Melt the butter and add to the mixture. Then add the parsley and Dijon mustard. Mix together and allow to cool.

Brown the steaks in a pan until they are a good colour. Season with salt and black pepper and spread the nut mixture on top of them. Bake them in a 200°C oven for about 8 mins.

Scald and seed the tomatoes, cut them into small cubes and fry them quickly in butter. Season with salt and pepper.

Take four good-shaped endive leaves and fry them quickly in the butter as well.

Cut each steak into three, put the pieces onto a plate and arrange an endive leaf filled with crushed tomato in the middle.

Veal noisettes with green asparagus and hollandaise sauce

To serve 4 persons

8 veal noisettes weighing about 35 g each
50 g butter
1 kg green asparagus
2 l water
1 tbsp coarse sea salt
1 tsp sugar
salt and freshly ground white pepper

For the hollandaise sauce,
see recipe on p. 64.

Prepare the sauce in advance and keep it warm.

Fry the noisettes in butter in a hot pan for 15 seconds on each side. Transfer them to an oven dish and season with salt and freshly ground white pepper. Heat the oven to 200°C.

Peel and cook the asparagus just before the meal begins. Place it in boiling water seasoned with salt and sugar. The right cooking time is about 8 mins from the point at which the water returns to the boil.

When the asparagus has been boiling for a couple of minutes, put the noisettes in the oven and cook for about 6 mins, until they are a rosé colour inside.

When the asparagus is ready al dente, take it out of the saucepan with a skimming ladle, wrap it in a clean teatowel and leave it to rest for a moment.

Arrange the asparagus and noisettes on the plate and pour hollandaise sauce over the asparagus.

Fried liver and steamed fennel with coriander sauce

To serve 4 persons

600 g veal or beef liver in slices
3 medium-sized bulbs of fennel
a drop of dry white wine
1 tsp finely chopped fresh tarragon
1 tsp finely chopped parsley

For the sauce
1 shallot
50 g butter
10 crushed coriander seeds
0.5 dl red wine
2 dl basic brown sauce
5 sprigs of fresh coriander
salt and freshly ground white pepper

Begin by preparing the sauce.

Chop the shallot and lightly fry it in butter. Add the coriander seeds and pour the red wine on top. Allow to boil for a moment, then add the brown sauce and sprigs of coriander. Cook over a gentle heat for about 10 mins and then sieve.

Cut the hard centres out of the fennel and slice the remainder into strips. Cook these in white wine over a gentle heat until they are al dente. Finally add the herbs and season with salt and pepper.

Fry the slices of liver in butter and season with salt and pepper.

Put them on a plate, pour the sauce over them and serve with the cooked fennel and good mashed potatoes if you wish.

Fillet of pork with beer sauce

To serve 4 persons

600 g fillet of pork, 150 g/person
12 slices of apple about 1 cm thick
120 g French beans
butter for frying

For the beer sauce
1 bottle of lager (0.3 l)
30 g butter
1 apple
1 shallot
10 whole white peppers
a drop of calvados
3 dl basic brown stock

Cut the pork fillet into four steaks, brown them in a frying pan and transfer them to an oven dish.

To prepare the sauce Peel and dice the apple.
Chop the shallot and lightly fry it in butter, add the cubes of apple and allow to soften for a moment. Add about half the beer and boil gently for some 10 mins. Reduce the mixture to a purée in a liquidizer and pour in the stock. Allow to boil for another 10 mins or so. Finally add a drop of calvados, sieve the sauce and season.

Place the pork fillets in a 200°C oven to cook for about 20 mins.

In the meantime, fry the apple rings in butter.

Top and tail the beans and cook them al dente in slightly salted water.

Put three apple rings on each plate, place a pork fillet on top of them and pour sauce around it. Serve with French beans.

SIMPLY DELICIOUS!

Two cooks on the waterfront

EERO MÄKELÄ AND I had dreamed of a restaurant of our own and discussed the matter so many times, in fact almost whenever we met, either at work or in our spare time – and that was quite often, as he was employed as a gastronomic consultant by a large hotel and restaurant organization and I was master chef at the Savoy, which was owned by the same company.

In 1993 the restaurant trade in Finland, like most other sectors of the economy, was struggling in the throes of a recession that had been going on for more than two years. Restaurants were having to close, even the best ones were laying off kitchen staff, and increasing numbers of tables were standing unoccupied from one evening to the next.

Although we were both happy in our work, the atmosphere was gradually getting us down and the idea of standing behind a stove of our own would come to mind increasingly often.

One rainy November morning fate took a hand in our affairs

On his way to work, Eero had stopped at the traffic lights on the north shore in the centre of Helsinki, and while waiting for them to change he noticed a large placard on the wall of one of the brick-built warehouses that stand on the opposite bank of the channel that separates the island of Katajanokka from the mainland. "Premises to rent", it read, followed by a telephone number. He managed to write the number down before the lights turned green.

It was common knowledge that these old redbrick warehouses that had been restored with care and devotion by a Helsinki property investor contained a fully furnished and equipped restaurant that was lying empty. It had three rooms decorated in different styles and a complete modern open kitchen with a glass wall through which diners could watch the

The man who met the First Lady. When Hillary Clinton visited Finland in 1996 she and her friends had lunch at Kanavaranta. On being served tar-flavoured ice-cream with spruce tip syrup, she praised it as "extremely interesting".

chefs at work. No one seemed to know whether it was the high rent or the predetermined furnishings that had discouraged potential restaurateurs, but another restaurant had been functioning continuously in the same building ever since the refurbishment was complete, and with great success.

Eero phoned me the same day and said that he had agreed to put in a bid for the premises over the coming weekend. Was I interested?

More or less there and then we set out to collect the keys and go to look at the restaurant. For the whole weekend we sat making calculations. Financial risks of this kind were something new for both of us.

"WE NEED A THIRD PARTNER – someone who can take care of the financial side and the day-to-day running of the business and all that that may entail." As soon as we had said this aloud, both of us knew who that third person might be.

We had known Maria Planting from the days of our cookery courses at the Palace and the Savoy, and we knew that she had also been on the famous Cordon Bleu course in Paris. She was indeed an "amatrice" in this field in the literal and most positive sense of the word. The most important thing from our point of view, however, was that, with her commercial training and experience as a reporter for the country's leading economic magazine, she had the necessary contacts. These were to prove immensely valuable later.

"This phone call may well turn out to be my best Christmas present this year", she said before we had even finished explaining our plans.

And so it was: in the beginning was a leasing contract, 178 empty chairs and three utterly inexperienced entrepreneurs

It was just before Christmas that we signed the contract that made us the first proprietors of this new, fully equipped and uniquely furnished restaurant, a restaurant with an image unprejudiced by the successes or calamities of past years. We could build up an institution in our own likeness, starting out from the quality of the food and service. We called our restaurant simply Kanavaranta, the Channel Bank.

ON THE DAY OF OUR PRESS CONFERENCE in January, the reporter, author and devotee of the culinary art Juha Tanttu wrote in his column in Helsingin Sanomat:

> "Today two Helsinki chefs, Eero Mäkelä and Gero Hottinger, will be telling the press about their new Kanavaranta Restaurant.
>
> Most Finnish master chefs prefer to remain anonymous, discreetly ensconced in their kitchens, but in this case the names of the chefs are more important than the name of the restaurant. It is these

that should be announced on the top of the menu and on the door.

We trust that Eero and Gero still believe as firmly as ever in the quality of Finnish fish and in the power of simplicity. Bread there must be, but not music – and preferably a bistro atmosphere rather than a businessmen's lunch philosophy. More important than chains or stars are customers who believe in creative cuisine. It is these, together with high aspirations on the part of the chefs, that can 'make' an eating place."

Goodness me, it was as if the man had read our thoughts!

IT WAS FEBRUARY 1994, the back of the recession had not yet been broken and not a single new restaurant had been opened in Helsinki for ages. We proposed to begin cautiously. We decided to practice first in just one of the three rooms a couple of weeks before the official opening of the restaurant. Our menu was fairly short but carefully thought out. We had baked our own bread, and the whole staff were dressed in traditional cooks' jackets and long, dark blue kitchen aprons – which was again something new in Finland.

We hadn't advertised very much, but relied on the fact that word would have spread around the city sufficiently for us to fill the forty places in our one room reasonably well. Even so, the excitement was intense in the time leading up to the first night, in the kitchens as well as the restaurant itself.

When the moment came, the room was full to the brim! And this continued, night after night. To our great sorrow, we had to turn people away during those first weeks, more people, in fact, than we were able to accommodate. The situation calmed down eventually, of course, but rumours went round for a long time that you could never find a free table at our restaurant.

Still more satisfying for us was our "failure of communication", the fact that few customers seemed to know the name of the restaurant but rumour had it that people in the city would simply say that they had been, or were going, to eat "at Eero and Gero's".

Kanavaranta bread

l litre orange juice
100 g yeast
1.5 dl home brewing malt
1.5 dl fine malt (for making Finnish *mämmi*)
3 dl rye flour
3 dl wheat bran
3 dl barley flour
about 10 dl wheat flour
1 tbsp salt
3 dl syrup

Warm the orange juice to hand heat and soak the yeast in it.

Mix all the ingredients together and allow the dough to rise for about 1.5 hours. The dough can be fairly runny.

Divide the dough between two long bread tins and bake in a 175°C oven for 1.5 hours. Baste the loaves with syrup when they have been in the oven for about an hour.

Lamb chops with goat's cheese, ratatouille and rosemary sauce

To serve 4 persons

12 lamb chops
12 slices of goat's cheese
salt and pepper
50 g butter for frying

For the ratatouille
1 small broccoli
1 small cauliflower
1 red pepper
1 small green pepper
100 g French beans
1 clove of garlic
olive oil
salt and pepper

For the rosemary sauce
2 shallots
20 g butter
1 dl red wine
3 whole branches of rosemary
4 dl basic brown stock
10 whole black peppers
1 tbsp cornflour

Begin by preparing the ratatouille.

Cut the peppers in half, remove the seeds and slice the flesh into about 1.5 cm pieces. Cut up the broccoli and cauliflower into thumb-tip sized florets and the French beans into pieces about 2 cm long.

Boil all these ingredients separately al dente.

Heat the olive oil in a saucepan, add the clove of garlic and allow to brown lightly. Then add all the vegetables and seasoning. Mix well and check for taste.

To prepare the sauce Finely chop the shallots and sauté them in butter. Add the red wine, rosemary branches and black pepper. Boil until practically all the liquid has evaporated. Add the stock and boil for about 15 mins.

Sieve the sauce and thicken with cornflour. Check the taste.

Fry the chops quickly in butter, transfer them to an oven tray and place a piece of goat's cheese on each. Cook in a 200°C oven for 6 mins.

Place a small heap of ratatouille on each plate, put the chops on top and pour the sauce around it.

Roast lamb with beans, French style

To serve 4 persons

4 small joints of roasting lamb weighing 150 g each
butter for frying
400 g French beans
3 tomatoes
2 shallots
2 small cloves of garlic
1 tbsp finely chopped parsley, rosemary and thyme
olive oil
salt and pepper from a mill

Brown the joints of lamb in a hot frying pan. When they are a beautiful brown on the surface, transfer them to an oven tray and season with salt and pepper.

Top and tail the beans and cook them al dente in salted water. Pour the water off and drop the beans into cold water to cool down. Then pour this water away as well.

Split the tomatoes in half, take out the seeds and cut the tomatoes into small strips. Peel and chop the shallots and cloves of garlic.

Roast the pieces of lamb for about 11 mins at 200°C.

While the meat is roasting, warm the olive oil a little in a large frying pan or wide, shallow saucepan, add the chopped shallots and garlic, allow these to cook for a moment and then add the beans. When the beans are hot, add the tomatoes and season with salt and pepper. Finally add the chopped herbs.

Slice the meat and serve with the beans and a red wine sauce (see recipe on p. 91).

Turkey saltimbocca

To serve 4 persons

8 thin slices of turkey breast
8 leaves of fresh sage
8 slices of Parma ham
50 g butter
1 dl dry white wine or marsala
salt
freshly ground white pepper
sage leaves for garnishing

Press the slices of turkey breast down until they are as thin as possible, place a slice of ham on each and a leaf of sage on top of this. Press these all together tightly with the fingers.

Melt the butter in a large pan, add the turkey breasts with the sage leaves pointing downwards. Fry well, turning them over from time to time, until the meat is browned on both sides.

Add the white wine, salt and pepper and allow to simmer under a cover for 6–8 mins, until the meat is cooked. Transfer the saltimboccas to a warmed serving dish.

Add a little water to the pan and allow it to boil for about a minute. Then pour this liquid on top of the saltimboccas.

Garnish with sage leaves and serve at once, e.g. with saffron rice.

Breast of wood pigeon with creamed savoy cabbage

To serve 4 persons

2 wood pigeons
a small savoy cabbage
100 g bacon
3 dl whipping cream
50 g butter
a sprinkling of nutmeg
salt and freshly ground white pepper

For the red wine sauce
1 shallot
10 g butter
1 dl red wine
6 whole white peppers
1/2 bay leaf
1 tbsp finely chopped parsley
3 dl basic brown stock
1 tsp arrowroot powder for thickening

Cut the breasts and legs from the wood pigeons, brown them quickly in a frying pan and place them on an oven tray.

Cut the savoy cabbage into strips and the bacon into pieces the size of a matchstick. Heat a saucepan and brown the bacon in it, add the cabbage, cover and allow to simmer for a moment. Warm the cream. Pour this into the saucepan and cook until the cabbage is soft and the sauce thick. Season with salt and pepper. Finally grind some nutmeg into the mixture and stir well.

To prepare the red wine sauce Finely chop the shallot and sauté it in butter for about a minute.

Add the red wine, peppers, bay leaf and chopped parsley and boil until the liquid has almost entirely evaporated.

Add the brown stock and cook for 10–15 mins. Sieve the sauce into another saucepan, season with salt as required and keep warm.

When the cabbage is done, roast the meat in a 200°C oven for 6 mins and serve out onto warmed plates at once. Garnish with the red wine sauce.

SIMPLY DELICIOUS!

"If only it were as much fun as this in every school!"

WE HAD PLANNED from the outset to arrange some small-scale cookery courses in connection with our restaurant, and when a suitable place for doing this became available on the floor above we couldn't resist the temptation, although the idea of another major project within such a short time was rather daunting.

Our aspiration was to turn our first Finnish cookery school into a permanent institution on the lines of Le Cordon Bleu or La Varenne, and this is why we gave it the fine-sounding name of the "Helsinki Culinary Institute".

This school intended for ordinary people who appreciate good food and all those interested in gastronomy began its first term in autumn 1994, with a course on sauces, which in fact became the favourite topic for a long time to come.

In the following years we took to arranging courses in the manner of a conventional school, with 6–7 new ones each autumn term and equally as many in the spring term. Most of the courses took place on Saturdays, lasted just under a day and were open to all those interested. It was possible to take 10–12 participants at a time, in order of application.

EACH COURSE ENDED with a dinner at which we ate the food that we had prepared during the day, accompanied by our choice of wines. There were mostly more applicants for a course than we could take, and so we often repeated the same course on the following Monday evening.

In between these courses we arranged small-scale demonstrations lasting a couple of hours in which Eero and I usually took turns to prepare a three-course meal in front of a full house of spectators.

WE ALSO INVITED "VISITING CELEBRITIES" to our school, beginning with Christian Guillut of Le Cordon Bleu and K. Karuna, a TV cook from Singapore, and continuing with the Swedish cookbook guru Carl Butler and many well-known Finnish master chefs.

Once we realized how well a day spent over the pots and pans helped people who had previously been complete strangers to get on together, we began tailoring courses individually for the clients of particular firms or other small groups of people. In fact these became so popular in time that nowadays we arrange the majority of our courses for companies or groups.

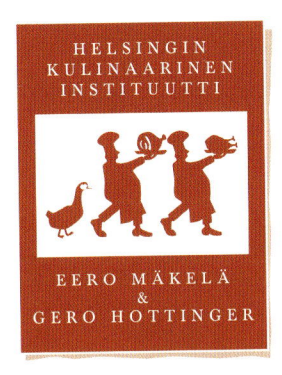

The logo that we devised for our restaurant and school came originally from a wrought-iron shop sign in Alsace. Many people have perceived a likeness between the figures in it and the three proprietors of Kanavaranta.

SIMPLY DELICIOUS!

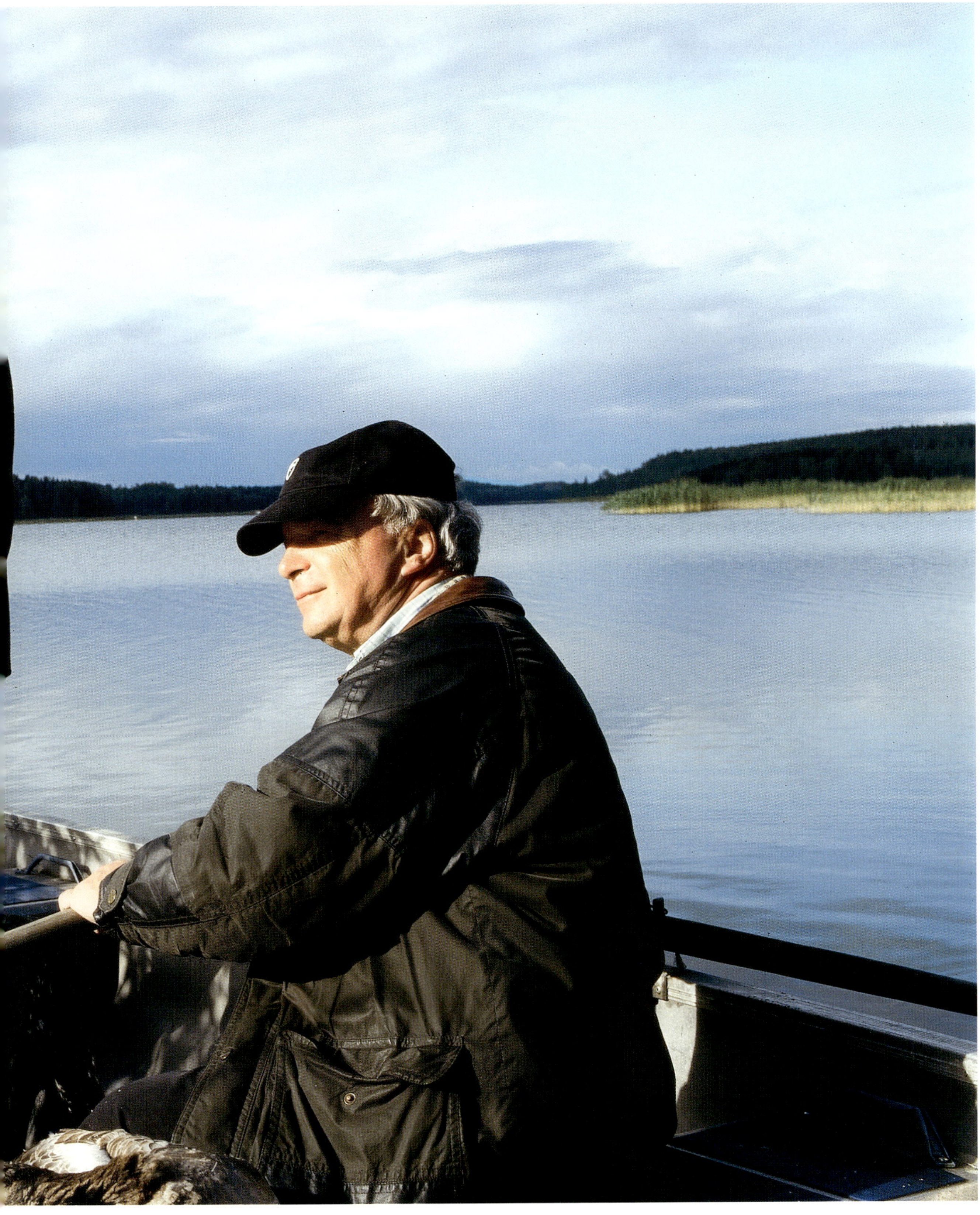

Whole roast wild duck with redcurrant sauce

To serve 4 persons

2 oven-ready ducks
1 carrot
1 small onion
2 bay leaves
3 dl basic brown stock
1 dl water
butter for frying
salt and freshly ground white pepper

For the redcurrant sauce
about 3 dl juice from the roasting of the ducks
1 dl whipping cream
1 tbsp redcurrant jelly
200 g fresh redcurrants
1 tsp blue cheese
cornflour for thickening
salt and white pepper from a mill

Redcurrants usually ripen conveniently for the beginning of the duck shooting season, and they provide a pleasantly sharp accompaniment to the traditional roast duck.

Rinse the ducks thoroughly and dry them well. Season them inside and out with salt and pepper.

Brown the ducks in butter and then place them in an oven dish together with the carrot and onion, cut into pieces, and the bay leaves.

Roast them for 10 mins in a 200°C oven first, then pour 1 dl cold water over them and roast for another 20 mins at 180°. After this, add the brown stock and continue cooking for about an hour, turning them from time to time.

When the ducks are cooked, lift them out of the dish and wrap them in aluminium foil. Sieve the juice left behind in the dish.

To prepare the redcurrant sauce Skim the fat off the top of the juice from the oven dish and boil the remainder until about 1 dl has evaporated.

Then add the cream, redcurrant jelly, fresh berries and blue cheese. Boil for about 5 mins and sieve. Thicken the sauce with cornflour mixed to a suitable consistency in a drop of water. Check the taste before serving.

Cut the ducks into pieces and serve with fried potatoes, sauce and redcurrant jelly.

Wild duck with apple and calvados sauce

To serve 4 persons

2 oven-ready ducks

For the apple and calvados sauce
- 6 apples
- 50 g butter
- 6 cl calvados
- 0.5 l red wine sauce
- salt and freshly ground white pepper
- a sprinkling of sugar

Remove the breasts and legs of the ducks, season with salt and freshly ground pepper and brown them quickly in butter in a frying pan. Then place them on an oven tray and cook them for about 16 minutes at 200°C, until they are of a rosé colour.

To prepare the sauce Peel and core the apples. Cut two of them into large cubes and fry them lightly in butter. Pour in about 4 cl of the calvados and boil for a moment. Add the red wine sauce (see p. 91) and cook until the apples are soft.

Reduce to a sauce in a liquidizer or with a hand blender in a saucepan. Bring to the boil again briefly and then sieve. Season with salt and freshly ground pepper.

Cut the remaining apples into small cubes (1 x 1 cm) and fry them in butter until soft. Then add the remaining calvados. Season with freshly ground pepper and a sprinkling of sugar.

Spread an even layer of sauce on a warmed plate and place one breast and one leg of duck on it together with a couple of spoonfuls of the diced apples.

Breast of willow grouse with white truffle and boletus sauce

To serve 4 persons

4 willow grouse breasts
8–10 small Boletus edulis mushrooms, about the size of the top joint of one's thumb

For the sauce

0.5 l basic brown stock
3 Boletus edulis mushrooms, chopped
1 tsp white truffle oil
1 dl whipping cream
2 sprigs of fresh thyme
1 small shallot
30 g butter
salt and freshly ground white pepper

To prepare the sauce Melt 20 g butter in a saucepan and sauté the chopped shallot. Add the chopped mushrooms and sprigs of thyme. Fry these lightly together for a couple of minutes, add the brown stock and boil for about 10 mins. Liquidize with a hand blender in a saucepan, add the truffle oil and whipping cream, season and pass through a sieve into another saucepan. Thicken a little if necessary.

Brown the willow grouse breasts rapidly in a small amount of butter, place them in an oven dish and cook in a 200°C oven for about 7 mins.

Slice the willow grouse breasts neatly and serve with sauce and the small mushrooms fried in butter.

Breast of duck flavoured with tea leaves and served with a potato cake and French beans

To serve 4 persons

2 duck breasts,
marinaded in the fridge for about 24 hours

For the marinade
2 tsp leaves of a scented tea,
e.g. Orange Pekoe or stronger
rind of 1 orange
2 tbsp rapeseed oil

For the sauce
20 g butter
1 shallot
2 whole cloves
juice of 1 orange
4 dl red wine sauce
1 tsp tea leaves (same variety as in the marinade)
salt and freshly ground black pepper

For the potato cakes
4 large, floury potatoes, e.g. Rosamunda
80 g butter
a little grated nutmeg
salt and freshly ground white pepper
200 g French beans

Mix the tea leaves with the oil. Peel the zest, or orange-coloured part of the rind, off the orange with a potato peeler or scraper intended for this purpose, cut it into wafer-thin strips and drop these into the oil.

Make deep, intersecting cuts with a sharp knife at about 1 cm intervals in the skin of the duck breasts, extending down to the fat layer. Place the breasts skin downwards in the marinade. Turn them from time to time.

To prepare the sauce Finely chop the shallot and sauté it in butter in a saucepan. Add the cloves and the juice squeezed from the orange and bring to the boil for a moment. Add the red wine sauce (see p. 91) and tea leaves and boil for about 10 mins. Finally sieve the sauce and season with salt and pepper.

To make the potato cakes Wash the potatoes and bake them in their jackets for about 50 mins in a 190°C oven.

Cut the potatoes open when cooked and removed the insides with a spoon. Add melted butter to this and season with nutmeg, salt and pepper. Form into disc-shaped cakes. Return these to the oven for a moment before serving.

Take the duck breasts out of the marinade and dry them with kitchen paper. Place them skin downwards in a cold frying pan and fry until the fat has melted out of them. Turn them over and fry them quickly on the other side. Season with salt and pepper.

Put the breasts in an oven dish and cook for about 14 mins at 200°C.

Place the meat on one side to rest for a moment after cooking and cut into slices with a sharp knife and divide into portions.

"Restaurant of the Year" after four years in business

AN UNKNOWN PHILOSOPHER, thinking aloud, once said,

"The world is full of learning, of clever scientists, skilful physicians, teachers and artists – but there are few who know how to run an inn properly."

Could the philosopher have been speaking from personal experience?

RUNNING AN "INN" is certainly anything but easy.

After practically a three-year "honeymoon" in the business, we gradually found ourselves coming up against the darker, everyday side of running a restaurant. We had certainly gained an established position as one of the best eating houses in town, but the initial novelty had worn off. People no longer queued for days to reach the delicacies on our counters, and the competition had become stiffer in terms of both the number of restaurants on offer and their quality. Although we tried our best at all times, there were many days on which nothing seemed to be going right either in the kitchens or in the restaurant itself.

WE HAD TRIED PRACTICALLY everything we could: the flambé evenings that were all the rage at that time, with considerable success at first, weekend brunch menus with slightly less success, and an outdoor terrace with still less, given the rainy weather during the summer and the shady and windswept aspect of our stretch of shore…

AND SO ONE DAY we simply decided that we had performed enough tricks. We vowed to go back to square one. We revised our menu once again, this time in the direction of good, honest basic food, we dusted down our wine cellar and improved the efficiency of both our kitchens and our service. It seems that we chose the right moment, too, for good quality food and service were beginning to gain recognition once again as economic circumstances improved.

ALTHOUGH WE WERE AWARE of the amount of work we had put in and of the fact that we were on the right track, we were highly surprised when the Finnish Gastronomical Society chose us as its Restaurant of the Year in 1998. The jury explained its choice in the following way: "Good Finnish food, high quality ingredients, respect for foods that are in season, elegant surroundings and friendly, well-informed service."

You can imagine how proud we were! Did we after all belong to the small band of those blessed with the knowledge of how to run an inn? Our more enthusiastic supporters began to look forward once again to the next Michelin Guide star awards.

Fillet of reindeer with endive and madeira sauce

To serve 4 persons

600 g reindeer fillet

Sauce
- 4 large endives
- 6 cl madeira
- 3 dl dark red wine sauce
- 50 g butter
- salt and freshly ground white pepper
- a sprinkling of sugar

Begin by preparing the sauce.

Cut the endives in two, remove the hard cores and cut the leaves into strips about 2 cm wide. Put 30 g of the butter into a broad, shallow pan and lightly sauté the endives for a moment. Add the madeira and boil for a while before pouring in the red wine sauce (see p. 91). Boil the sauce a little longer, to thicken, and then season with salt, pepper and a sprinkling of sugar.

Brown the fillets of reindeer quickly in butter in a frying-pan, season them with salt and pepper and cook them in a 200°C oven for about 4 mins (or slightly longer, depending on their size), until they are a rosé colour inside.

Place a pool of endive sauce in the centre of each plate and arrange slices of meat around it.

Rosé-roasted fillet of reindeer with juniper berry sauce and potato and boletus hash

To serve 4 persons

600 g fillet of reindeer

For the sauce
1 shallot
15 g butter
1 dl red wine
1 tbsp chopped parsley stems
12 juniper berries
4 whole white peppers
4 dl basic brown stock
some cornflour or barley thickening

For the boletus hash
300 g diced boletus mushrooms
300 g boiled potatoes, diced
1 shallot
2 tbsp finely chopped parsley
salt and freshly ground white pepper
butter for frying

Season the meat with salt and black pepper and brown it in butter. Place it in the oven at 200°C and cook for about 8 mins.

To prepare the sauce Chop the shallot and sauté it in butter. Add the red wine, parsley stems, crushed juniper berries and white peppers. Boil until the liquid has almost entirely evaporated away.

Add the brown stock and cook for about 10 mins. Sieve the sauce into another saucepan and thicken with cornflour or barley thickening. Check the taste at the end.

To prepare the hash Sauté the shallot in butter and then add the mushrooms.

Once the mushrooms have changed colour, pour in the diced potatoes and fry these together for a moment. Season and add the finely chopped parsley.

Not just any hamburger steak

ONION STEAK *(Pannbiff med lök)* and Lindström's steak *(Biff à la Lindström,* the one made with half minced meat and half beetroot, adding onion and capers), are without doubt among the best-known ordinary everyday dishes in Sweden – and they have become very popular nowadays in Finland, too. They were quite acceptable for a luncheon even at the Grand Hôtel in Stockholm, although they wouldn't have been condoned on a dinner menu however highly one might regard minced meat steaks as such.

Wallenbergare is an entirely different matter, of course. The very name sound much finer than "minced meat" or "hamburger", and the steak itself is far more delicious than it looks.

THE ORIGINAL RECIPE is said to have been created by Charles Emil Hagdahl, an excellent doctor and notable writer on cookery, some time at the end of the 19th century. The fact that his daughter married into the mighty Wallenberg banking family may have had something to do with the name he chose for his fine steak.

The original Wallenbergare has boiled sweetbreads ground into the mixture as well as leg of veal, which give it its light, mild taste. This was the recipe used at the Grand Hôtel in my time:

To serve 4 persons

400 g finely ground leg of veal
100 g boiled sweetbreads, finely cut
4 egg yolks
3 dl cold whipping cream
salt and pepper
finely grated and sieved white bread
(mie de pain)

A genuine Wallenbergare should be served in the traditional manner, with mashed potatoes, boiled peas and crushed lingonberries *(Vaccinium vitis-ideae).*

Innumerable variations on this delightful theme have arisen in the course of time, including elegantly prepared fish or pheasant Wallenbergare, which have transformed the Swedes' beloved everyday luncheon dish into a delicacy for the finest of dinner menus. The following is an interesting variation using Finnish elk steak, and the classic Wallenbergare can also be made from the same recipe.

Elk Wallenbergare

To serve 4 persons

400 g minced elk meat
200 g minced pork
6 egg yolks
3–4 dl ice-cold whipping cream
salt
freshly ground white pepper
a little nutmeg
4 dl grated fresh white bread, mie de pain
melted butter for frying

Put the elk meat and pork in a bowl and stand this in a large vessel filled with ice cubes. Mix the meat together in the bowl, add the seasoning and the egg yolks one by one. Then add the cream in small amounts, stirring constantly.

Put the bowl in the fridge for a moment.

On taking it out, form the minced meat mixture into large steaks, dip them carefully into the breadcrumbs and fry them slowly in butter in a moderately hot pan.

Serve at once with boiled peas, mashed potatoes and crushed lingonberries with a little sugar added.

Elk meat goulash with spätzle

To serve 4 persons

1 kg elk steak,
marinaded for a day beforehand

For the marinade
1 carrot, sliced
80 g celeriac, diced
1 chopped shallot
3–4 stems of parsley
8 juniper berries
2 bay leaves
3 dl red wine

For the sauce
1.5 l game stock
50 g butter
cornflour for thickening
salt and freshly ground black pepper

For the spätzle
300 g flour
3 eggs
1 dl water
a little salt

Begin by making the marinade in a deep, wide dish. Put the vegetables and seasoning on the bottom and pour the red wine and a drop of water onto them. Cut the meat into pieces about 3 x 3 cm.

Drop the meat into the marinade and allow to stand in the fridge overnight.

Take the meat out of the marinade and sieve the liquid. Keep the slices of carrot on one side.

Brown the pieces of meat in butter in a saucepan and pour in the game stock and half the liquid from the marinade. Allow to simmer gently and then add the slices of carrot. When the meat is done, season the sauce and thicken with cornflour.

To prepare the spätzle This traditional "pasta" from the Schwaben area of South Germany is an excellent accompaniment to game or meat stews – and, what is more, it is easy to make.

Put the flour in a bowl and add the eggs. Stir with a wooden spoon and add the water and salt. Stir hard until distinct bubbles can be seen. Squeeze the dough through a spätzle maker or a coarse sieve into a large quantity of vigorously boiling salt water.

Cook the spätzle for about 2 mins, until it rises to the surface of the water. Then lift it out onto a plate with a skimming ladle.

Fry the spätzle in butter just before serving.

SIMPLY DELICIOUS!

A time – and a place – for everything

Eero and Gero in the kitchen of the Kanavaranta Restaurant.

AS THE FIRST YEAR of the new millennium drew to a close we knew that we had a difficult decision ahead of us.

Eero was about to go into well-deserved retirement, and we knew from experience that it would be an overwhelming job in the long run, even with two chefs, to keep up the restaurant and the school as they were – not to mention expanding them. I nevertheless decided to continue alone, at least for the time being.

When a little more than a year had passed, however, the idea of closing the restaurant altogether began to seem a more and more reasonable alternative. I was inclined to think that it was best to "step out of the ring" while we were still in the top rank. I had already decided to carry on with the Culinary Institute in new premises in the city centre.

Needless to say, it was a rather nostalgic moment when our last night had drifted into the early hours of the morning and it was time to put the lights out in our Kanavaranta kitchens for the last time.

Even master chefs feel tired – sometimes

As workplaces go, the kitchens of even the finest restaurants are seldom a heaven – in fact they are far more often hot and sweaty like the cellars of that horned and forked-tailed devil. Sixteen-hour days are more the rule than the exception, especially for a cook who is slaving over his own stove, and although we master chefs are a rare breed who have adapted remarkably well to this odd form of existence, I have seen many of my colleagues utterly worn out far too early in life.

Thus it is always a great thing to see companions who have put in a good stint going into well-earned retirement still in full possession of their mental and physical faculties – even though it sometimes means the end of a long-lasting working relationship.

RETIREMENT GAVE EERO a chance to work shorter days and spend more time on other things that interested him, on writing, travel and many other connections that he still has with the culinary profession.

Eero Mäkelä must still be the best-known master chef in Finland, partly because he has guided so many of the younger generation in the secrets of the trade in the course of the years. Indeed, one could very well say that the talented chefs of today are "reaching for the stars" largely by following in his footsteps.

If the perceptive reader has sensed in the recipes in this book a little of the "harmony of tastes" so characteristic of Eero's work, then I can simply be unreservedly proud of the fact.

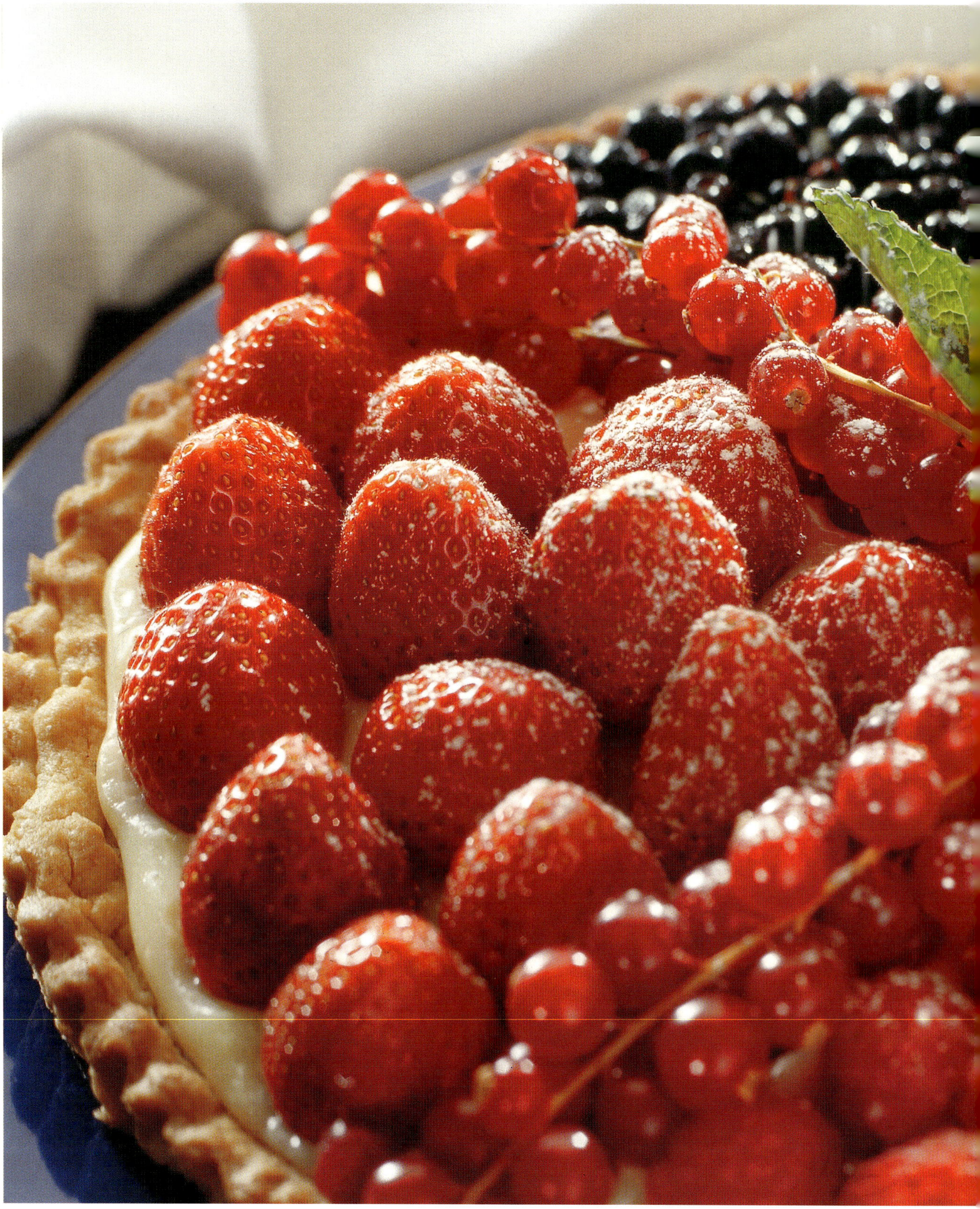

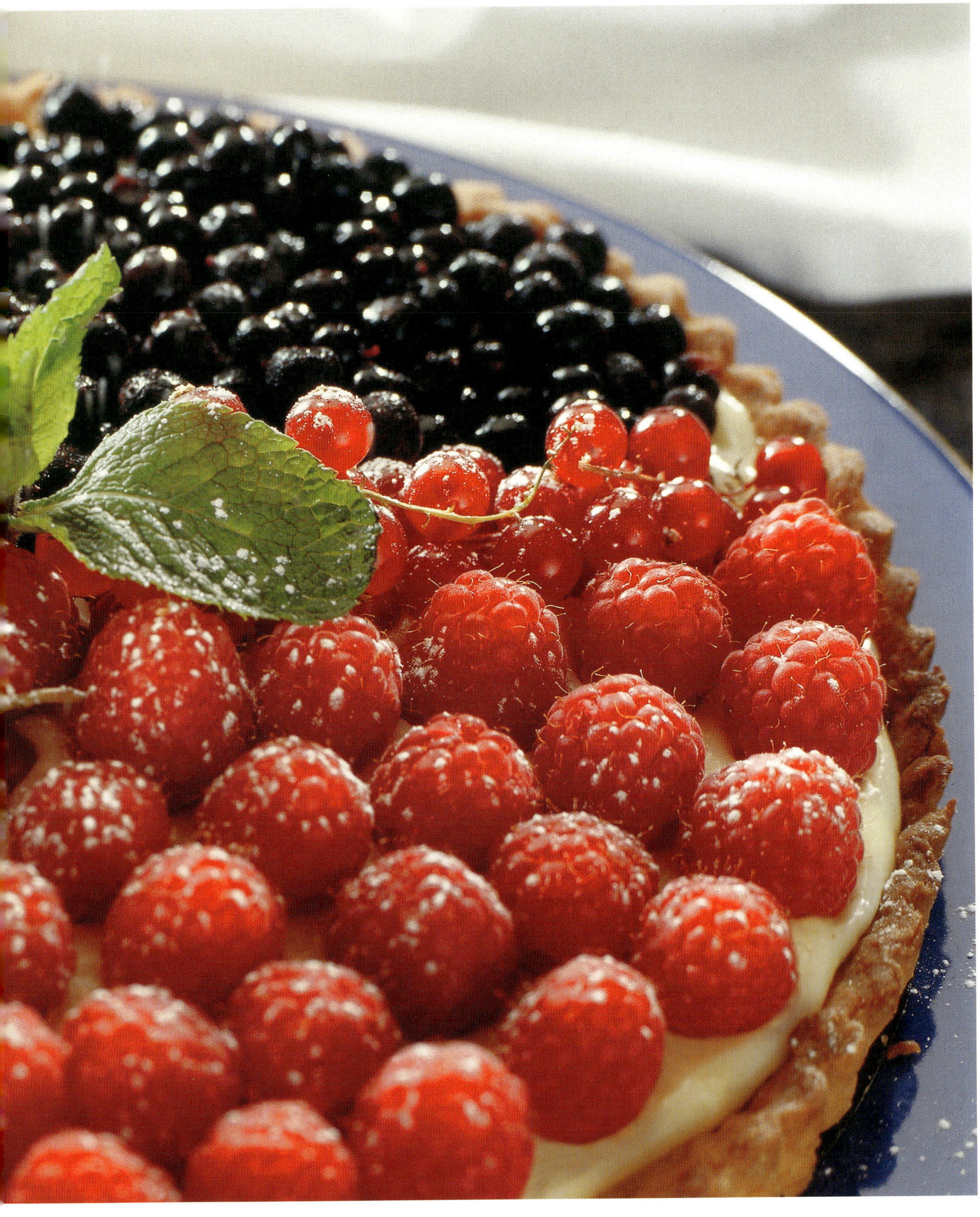

Apple pastries with rapsberry sauce

To serve 4 persons

For the pastry
- 4 slabs of ready-made puff pastry, each about 6 x 10 cm
- a sheet of greaseproof paper
- 1 egg
- 2 apples
- 2 tbsp sugar
- cinnamon and icing sugar

For the sauce
- 200 g fresh raspberries
- 2 tbsp sugar
- water

To make the pastry base Heat the oven to 190°C. Roll out the pastry slabs to a thickness of about 3 mm and lay them on greaseproof paper on an oven tray.

Peel and core the apples and cut into slices.

Paint the pastry lightly with beaten egg and cover with slices of apple. Sprinkle with a little cinnamon and icing sugar.

To make the sauce Reduce the raspberries to a sauce with the sugar and a drop of water in a blender. Sieve and serve with the apple pastries.

Orange cheesecake

To serve 4 persons

a large baking dish, diameter 24 cm,
or four small ones, diameter 8 cm
a sheet of greaseproof paper
20 digestive biscuits
80 g butter
4 leaves of gelatine
200 g mascarpone or other fresh cheese
1 egg, separated into yolk and white
60 g fructose
1.5 dl orange juice
4 cl Grand Marnier liqueur
3 dl whipping cream
a little cocoa powder for dusting

Grind the biscuits in a blender and add the melted butter.

Cut a piece of greaseproof paper to fit the bottom of the baking dish, so that the cheesecake can be taken out more easily for serving. Press the biscuit mixture down firmly to form an even layer on the bottom of the dish.

Soak the leaves of gelatine in cold water for about 10 mins.

Whisk the egg yolk and half the fructose into the cheese. Mix the other half of the fructose with the egg white and beat to a firm froth.

Heat the orange juice, add the Grand Marnier liqueur and the leaves of gelatine and heat again until the gelatine has entirely dissolved. Take the saucepan off the heat.

Then add the cheese mixture and whipped cream. Pour the filling onto the base of crushed biscuits and put the whole cheesecake into the fridge to cool.

Sprinkle cocoa powder on the cheesecake just before serving.

Rhubarb tiramisu

For the rhubarb jelly
- 1 l rhubarb, peeled and cut into pieces about 1 cm long
- 3 dl caster sugar
- 3 dl water
- 1 dl Triple Sec liqueur
- 4 leaves of gelatine
- a steep-sided oven dish (12 x 25 cm)

For the mascarpone mixture
- 4 egg yolks
- 4 egg whites
- 100 g sugar (less if you don't like things so sweet)
- a sprinkling of vanilla sugar
- 400 g mascarpone cheese
- 2 tbsp cognac or other brandy

To make the rhubarb jelly Put the gelatine leaves into cold water to soak for about 10 mins.

Put the other ingredients in a saucepan to simmer gently until the rhubarb begins to soften.

Take the saucepan off the stove and add the gelatine, stirring all the time. Pour the mixture into the oven dish and put it in the fridge to set.

To make the cheese mixture Whisk the sugar, egg yolks and vanilla sugar to a pale froth. Cream the mascarpone a little at room temperature, add it to the mixture and stir well. Add the brandy. Whip the egg whites to a firm froth and fold into the mixture carefully in 3–4 portions.

Spread the mascarpone mixture onto the rhubarb layer and return the dish to the fridge until the time comes for serving it.

Strawberry surprise

To serve 4 persons

about 300 g fresh strawberries

For the hazelnut biscuits
 1 egg white
 40 g sugar
 50 g finely chopped hazelnuts
 a sheet of greaseproof paper

For the mascarpone filling
 2 eggs
 50 g sugar
 3 tbsp Triple Sec liqueur
 100 g mascarpone cheese
 grated rind of half an orange
 1.5 dl whipped cream
 some fresh leaves of mint and
 icing sugar for decoration

To make the biscuits Whisk the egg white and some of the sugar to a froth. Add the chopped hazelnuts and the remainder of the sugar and stir well.

Heat the oven to 170°C. Spread the greaseproof paper on an oven tray and shape the mixture into 8 slabs of about 8 x 8 cm on it. Bake these for about 15 mins and take them out to cool.

For the filling Mix the egg yolks with the sugar and then pour in the liqueur. Add the mascarpone and stir well. Then mix in the grated orange rind and whipped cream.

Finally beat one of the egg whites until stiff and fold it carefully into the cheese mixture. You can add a little sugar if you wish.

Put a biscuit on the plate, cover with filling and top with fresh strawberries, then cover with a second biscuit and more filling and strawberries.

Decorate these "surprises" with fresh leaves of mint and a sprinkling of icing sugar.

Summer berry tart

a baking dish of diameter 28 cm
butter for greasing the dish
500 g oven-ready shortcrust pastry
fresh strawberries
fresh raspberries
fresh bilberries
fresh redcurrants

For the filling
2.5 dl milk
3 egg yolks
80 g sugar
8 cl citrus liqueur
40 g cornflour
icing sugar for dusting

Begin by preparing the filling.

Bring the milk to the boil in a saucepan. Mix the egg yolks, sugar and cornflour together well and pour the mixture into the milk. Return just to the point of boiling, stirring all the time. When the mixture has thickened, take the saucepan off the heat, add the liqueur and allow to cool.

Carefully roll out the pastry. Grease the baking dish and spread the pastry on it. Bake in a 185°C oven and allow to cool.

Spread the filling evenly over this base and arrange the berries on top in groups. Finally dust the surface with icing sugar.

Crème brûlée with cloudberries

To serve 8 persons

6 dl whipping cream
0.5 dl cloudberry liqueur
1.5 dl milk
1 vanilla pod
1 dl sugar
8 egg yolks
0.5 dl caster sugar for caramelizing
fresh cloudberries for decoration

Heat the oven to 100–125°C.

Bring the cream, milk, split vanilla pod and half the sugar to the boil in a saucepan.

Whisk the egg yolks and the remainder of the sugar to a light-coloured froth, pour the cream mixture and the liqueur into this and serve out into shallow china bowls about 15 cm in diameter.

Place the bowls in water in the oven and cook for about 30 mins.

Before taking the bowls of custard out of the oven prod them with a knife to check that they are cooked all through. Allow to cool well (preferably in a fridge overnight).

When they are suitably cold, sprinkle caster sugar on the surface and place into a hot oven until this sugar has melted entirely to form a caramel layer.

Cool again and top with sugared cloudberries.

A dessert trio

White chocolate tart with redcurrant jelly,
chocolate expresso fondant and chocolate soufflé in a glass

To serve 4 persons

1. White chocolate tart with redcurrant jelly

For the redcurrant jelly
    1 dl redcurrant juice
    1 dl water
    50 g sugar
    2 leaves of gelatine

For the white chocolate base
    120 g white chocolate
    2 leaves of gelatine
    3 dl whipping cream
    1 egg
    3 tbsp Triple Sec liqueur

To make the redcurrant jelly Bring the redcurrant juice, water and sugar to the boil in a saucepan. When the sugar has dissolved entirely, add the gelatine leaves after soaking them in cold water for some time. Boil, stirring carefully with a spoon, until the gelatine has melted completely. Pour the liquid into a deep dish about 16 cm in diameter and put it in the fridge to set.

To make the white chocolate base Soak the leaves of gelatine in cold water and melt the white chocolate gently over warm water. Whisk the cream and beat the egg separately to a froth. Heat the liqueur in a saucepan, add the gelatine and heat further, stirring carefully, until the gelatine has melted.

Mix the beaten egg into the melted chocolate and then add the liqueur with the dissolved gelatine in it. Stir until the mixture is smooth and then add the whipped cream, still stirring well.

Pour on top of the redcurrant jelly, smoothe the surface over carefully, cover the dish with cling foil and return to the fridge for about 4 hours.

To serve, loosen the edges of the tart from the dish with a thin-bladed knife and then place the whole dish in warm water for a moment. After that it should be easy to turn the tart out onto a plate. Cut into portions of the desired size.

2. Chocolate expresso fondant

See the recipe for four pieces on p. 125.

3. Chocolate soufflé in a glass

Prepare the soufflé last, immediately before serving.

    4 eggs
    80 g soft butter
    80 g icing sugar
    120 g dark chocolate (at least 70% cocoa)
    soft butter and sugar for lining the glass
    icing sugar for dusting
    4 small, steep-sided glasses (size about 12 cl)

Separate out the egg whites and yolks. Whip the butter and sugar to a paste and add the egg yolks one at a time.

Melt the chocolate over warm water and add to the mixture. Whisk the egg whites to a froth and fold them gently into the chocolate mixture.

Smear the inner surfaces of the glasses with butter and sprinkle them with an even coating of sugar.

Fill the glasses 2/3 full with the soufflé mixture, place them in water and cook in a 200°C oven for about 18 mins.

Serve the soufflé in the glasses, with a little icing sugar sprinkled on top.

The dessert can be decorated with a few redcurrants or other fresh berries.

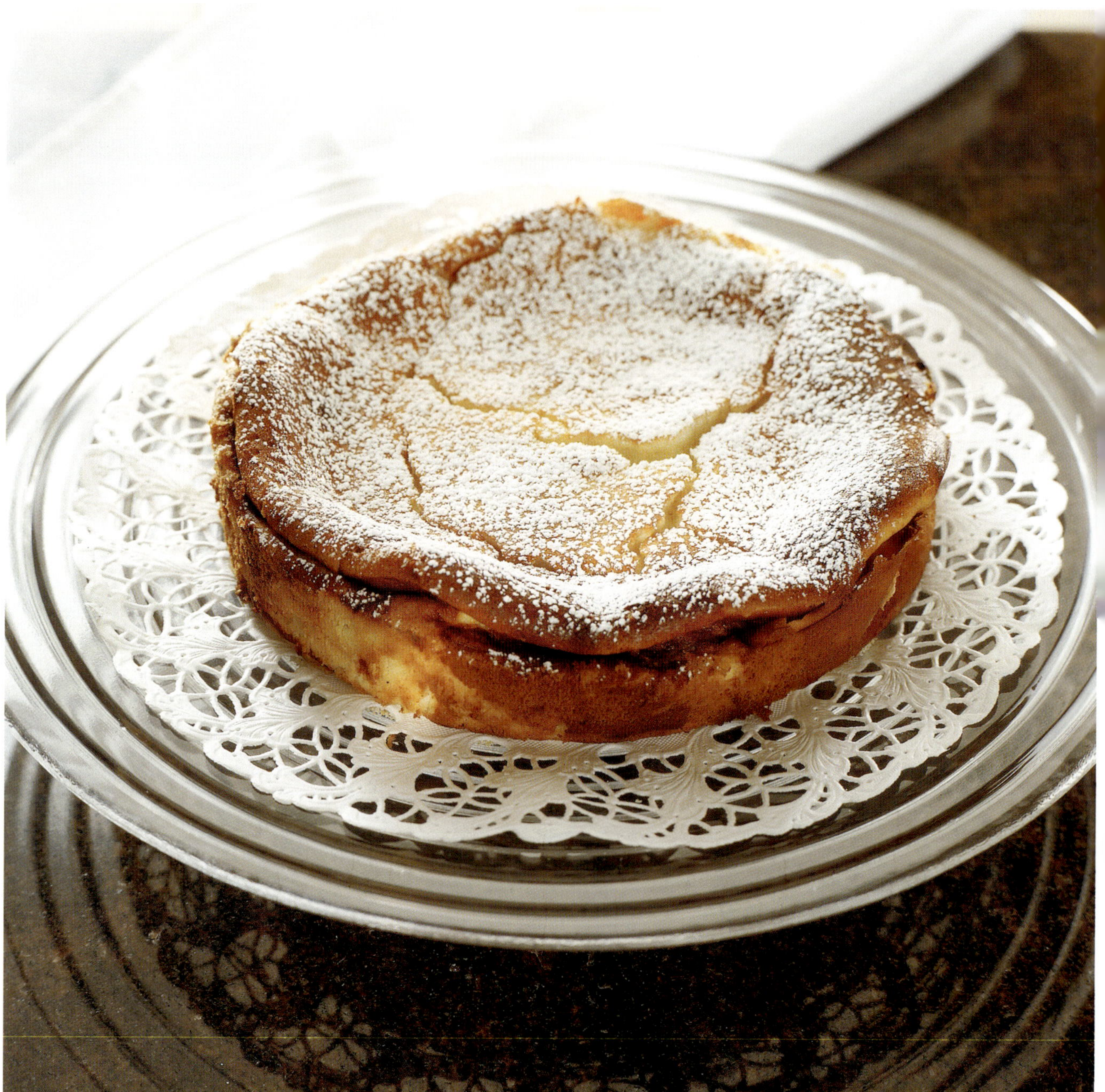

The unforgettable tart

AS FAR AS I KNOW, I first made the acquaintance of this tart on my 5th birthday. In fact, I can't remember anything else about the whole event except that my grandmother had baked a tart that to my childhood taste was quite unbelievably delicious.

And that same tart has been a more or less recurrent feature of my life ever since. It has always appeared on the table when something important has happened to me: a birthday, my first communion, when I qualified as a chef, or when I came out of the army.

First it was my grandmother who made it for me, then my mother, and later my wife learned the secret of it. I sometimes make it myself, true, but it never seems to taste quite right unless someone else has made it for me.

I remember how important it was when we were children for my brother and I to keep an eye on the tart as it rose, and to put our noses up to a chink in the oven door, sometimes a little too enthusiastically, to get the first whiff of it as it was baking. Seldom has an hour dragged past so slowly as when we were waiting for that tart to cook!

When it was ready and had risen to a magnificent round shape on top, the hot tart would usually be put in front of a partially open window in the kitchen or dining room to cool and stand. It was important to shut the door to the room, though, so that there wouldn't be any draught that might cause the tart to sink unexpectedly, for it was just as temperamental and unpredictable as a cheese soufflé. Even so, in spite of all the precautions, the tart would sometimes collapse before our very eyes, and I am certain that I could detect a faint hiss of air escaping from its insides as it did so.

I HAVE LEARNED through age and experience that this regrettable calamity happens on about one occasion in three, but fortunately it doesn't affect the taste of the tart at all!

What on earth is it, then, that makes this ordinary quark tart so extraordinary? Evidently we have to face up once again to one of the basic truths of "the physiology of taste". We don't savour things only with the taste buds on our tongue but with all our senses – and to quite a considerable extent with our memory as well!

The best quark tart of my childhood days

750 g quark
250 g sugar
70 g butter
6 eggs
1 tbsp semolina
1 tbsp flour
grated rind of a lemon
30 g vanilla sugar
icing sugar

Separate the egg yolks from the whites. Whisk the yolks and sugar to a foam, pour in the other ingredients and stir well. Finally whisk the egg whites to a froth and fold in carefully.

Bake the tart in a vertical-sided, openable cake tin of diameter 28 cm for about 50 mins at 170°C.

Allow it to cool before taking it out of the tin. Dust generously with icing sugar.

Chocolate expresso fondant

To serve 4 persons

200 g dark chocolate (70% cocoa)
3.5 dl whipping cream
1 dl espresso or coffee liqueur
cocoa powder for dusting
greaseproof paper

Take a shallow, vertical-sided baking dish or four small ring moulds. Cut the greaseproof paper to cover the bottom(s) well.

Melt the chocolate over moderately warm water. Bring 0.5 dl of the whipping cream to the boil, add the liqueur and mix these ingredients into the chocolate. Allow the mixture to cool to hand temperature.

Whisk the remainder of the cream to a froth and fold into the chocolate.

Fill the baking dish or moulds with the chocolate mixture, smoothe the surface well and place in the fridge for at least 4 hours.

To serve, run a thin knife round the edge of the dish or mould to loosen the fondant and turn it out onto a plate. Remove the paper and sprinkle cocoa powder onto the surface through a sieve.

The old manor house and its young staff in summer 2004, a fine team who have blended together well from the beginning.

Spring comes to the innkeeper

WE COOKS ARE a strange bunch of people. We don't have to be away from our hot stoves for more than a brief moment before we feel a tremendous desire to be back at work, even though there might be far easier ways of earning a living.

I had admittedly had my ears open for some time for an opportunity to start a restaurant of my own again, but once more the eventual break came quite by chance.

I heard that the local council of Lempäälä in Häme was looking for a restaurateur for the Villa Hakkari manor house which it owned, and the idea seemed appealing, especially as I was not inclined to open yet another new restaurant in Helsinki, where the market was already overcrowded. And so I decided to drop by in Lempäälä.

I WAS SOLD ON THE IDEA at my first visit. The 200-year-old Empire-style manor house and its extensive gardens are located in a beautiful spot very close to the centre of Lempäälä and only just over ten kilometres from Tampere. The outside of the house was admittedly in need of a coat of paint and its halls and six little side rooms obviously had to be thoroughly redecorated, but otherwise the place seemed ideal.

I said that I would like to begin with a good lunch to celebrate May Day. Was it possible to have the repair work finished in just under five months?

The people of Häme have a reputation for being slow, but this is not always the case, the elders of Lempäälä District Council assured me.

WHEN LUNCHTIME on the First of May came round, the house was full to the last seat, and we decided there and then that the following year we would arrange two sittings for lunch so that we could accommodate everyone who wanted to come.

I have already settled down and made myself at home in Lempäälä, and the hen that I was given as an arriving present seems to be highly contented and growing fatter day by day in the care of my neighbour.

SIMPLY DELICIOUS!

Ravintola
VILLA HAKKARI

Meny

Haalea kantarellisalaatti

Tuorepaprika-tomaattikeitto
vuohenjuuston kera

Pinjansiemenillä
ja pistaasimanteleilla
päällystetty entrecôte

Suomalaisia juustoja

Mansikkayllätys

"Gero, tell us the proper way to plan a menu."

I THINK I MUST HAVE BEEN asked this at least once on every course at the Culinary Institute – regardless of whether we are supposed to be learning about sauces, desserts or whatever it is. Unfortunately it has seldom been possible to do justice to the request, as it is not easy to devise a stylish and well balanced meal just like that – let alone teach someone else how to do it in a ten-minute off-the-cuff lecture! Even now we shall have to be content with a couple of pages of ideas on the subject, although it would really warrant a whole book.

Apart from the taster menus that have become popular at some gourmet restaurants, it is rare nowadays to serve more than six courses even at the finest dinners – usually there are only three or four. The order of courses, however, tends still to follow the time-honoured pattern.

1.
Hors d'oeuvres (Starter)
2.
Hot fish course
3.
Entremets
4.
Hot meat course
5.
Cheese course
6.
Dessert

IN THIS SCHEME the starter is usually something other than fish and the entremets following the hot fish course is nowadays mostly a refreshing sorbet that is intended to whet the appetite for the highlight of the whole meal, the meat course and the wine to be served with it.

Let's look at an example before we say any more about food and wine. A five-course meal can be planned using entirely recipes to be found on the pages of this book.

Menu I

Warm chanterelle salad
(p. 22)

Sweet pepper and tomato soup with goat's cheese
(p. 40)

Entrecôte steaks with stone pine seeds and pistachios
(p. 78)

Selection of Finnish cheeses
(goat's cheese, black label Emmental and Tilsit)

Strawberry surprise
(p. 117)

Wines

Pinot Gris
Bordeaux
Finnish strawberry liqueur

I HAVE CHOSEN specifically late summer delicacies for this menu, and ones that represent a short circular tour from Finland to the shores of the Mediterranean and back.

It is also important to consider the sizes of the portions, however, so that the journey will not be too arduous. The more courses you plan, the smaller the portions will have to be.

AND WHAT ABOUT THE WINES, then? Mushrooms are known to go well with wine. In this case the combination of fried chanterelles and bacon will soften the slight acidity of the salad dressing very nicely, and as Pinot Gris white wines are good all-purpose wines that can be served with many kinds of food, we could choose here a dry Italian Pinot Grigio or a demi-sec Tokay-Pinot Gris from Alsace.

A dry Pinot Gris would also be suitable with the sweet pepper and tomato soup, although I don't especially recommend wine with soups; it is often better to go for mineral water or iced water. One exception, though, concerns full-bodied creamy mushroom soups, with which dry sherry or white port is excellent, while a

SIMPLY DELICIOUS!

Ravintola VILLA HAKKARI

Meny

Kylmäsavuporonpaistia
ja naurispaistosta

Paistettu kuhafilee
vihannesratatouillea ja
rosmariinikastiketta

Omenalehikäinen ja
vadelmakastiketta

glass of sparkling wine serves well to bring out the flavour of crayfish or prawn soups or to reinforce that of soups already containing sparkling wine or champagne.

The entrecôte will call for a moderately full-bodied red wine. AC Bordeaux Supérieur would be very suitable, for instance, or a Médoc if you want to choose a château wine.

In this case I chose one of our many excellent Finnish berry liqueurs to go with the strawberry surprise rather than a sweet wine. These are often made nowadays at small wineries in the countryside as well as by larger industrial producers. Sweet berry liqueurs to accompany desserts should always be well chilled before serving.

Menu II

Cold-smoked reindeer with baked turnip
(p. 26)

Fried fillet of pike-perch, ratatouille and rosemary sauce
(p. 58)

Apple pastries with raspberry sauce
(p. 114)

Wines

Côtes du Rhône
Asti Tosti

THIS THREE-COURSE LUNCH OR DINNER menu uses ingredients that are readily available all year round, although to my palate it has a special taste of late summer or early autumn. The ratatouille and rosemary sauce add a small southern European touch to the palette of otherwise typically Finnish flavours.

A good luncheon wine for drinking throughout the meal would be an AC-class white Côtes du Rhône or a Viognier from the Pays d'Oc region.

For a dinner it would be possible to serve a more full-bodied Châteauneuf-du-Pape, for instance, or a Hermitage – both of them Rhône wines.

A sweet Italian Asti Tosti spumante would crown the dessert course.

First the food and then the wines

When planning a menu it is always good to start with the food and to make sure that the various courses blend together well. Only when you believe that you have arrived at an interesting and harmonious overall menu is it time to move on to consider the wines.

The same rules nevertheless apply to both the choice of courses for the meal and the choice of wines to accompany it: mild flavours should come before powerful ones, dry wines before sweet ones, fish before meat, white wine before red, light meat before dark. And the fullness of the tastes should increase towards the end of the meal.

The finest wine is not always the most suitable! As a cook, I naturally want the ingredients and aromas of the dishes I have prepared to stand out as well as possible, and wines can be both friends to the food and its worst competitors. The most difficult thing of all to my mind is to plan the menu for a meal at which the master of the house intends to fill the glasses with the most precious wines that he has been cherishing in his cellars over the years. All you can do in such a situation is remember the old rule of thumb: keep it simple, but good. Give a great wine the chance to be queen for the evening!

SIMPLY DELICIOUS!

1. A stainless steel saucepan is essential for many purposes, and one should have two or three of them at hand, and similarly stainless steel or ceramic baking dishes.

2. One good stainless steel whisk will go a long way, but you should have another one, of wood or plastic, for use in Teflon saucepans.

3. You will probably need sieves of several sizes and shapes.

4. You will need various sizes of rings and moulds both for baking and for shaping potato cakes, vegetable terrines etc.

5. As well as a plastic-headed spatula, you will probably find use for a couple of wooden spoons and slices.

6. A classic carving fork is an excellent help when carving poultry or joints of meat.

Cooking is a matter of skill, not of equipment

THE MOST MODERN RESTAURANT kitchens seem to be full of instrumentation, like the cockpit of a jumbo jet, and even home cooks seem to try their utmost to keep up with the latest technological developments. If I were a home cook, I would invest in a really good oven rather than collecting all manner of magic devices.

Of the household appliances, a universal mixer or a liquidizer can be a great benefit – but even then a hand-held blender may be quite sufficient. I rather suspect, in fact, that the majority of the other machines tend to be consigned to the corner of a cupboard to gather dust after being used a few times.

7. An asparagus peeler can be useful for peeling potatoes and root vegetables as well.

8. This corer can be used for taking the core and pips out of apples, for instance.

9. A zest scraper is used for taking the thin surface layer, or zest, off an orange or lemon to flavour a sauce or dessert or for decorative use.

10. A cutter wheel can be used to cut pasta dough into squares or strips, for instance.

11. A good pair of kitchen scissors that sit comfortably in the hand are an essential.

12. A stout pair of pliers can be useful for pulling the larger bones out of a salmon or other fish.

13. If you have a couple of decilitre or two-decilitre measures there's no need to guess the amounts of liquid or flour.

A COOK NEEDS A GOOD SET OF KNIVES, however. Three or four will be enough, provided they are kept meticulously sharpened. A blunt knife is not only useless but also dangerous, and a real cook will never put the best kitchen knives in the dishwasher!

The tools of the trade for a cook are simple and well tried over countless generations. Those that I use for preparing the dishes described in this book are practically all here – bar the pasta maker and smoking box.

WHAT KIND OF SALT AND PEPPER should one use? I personally use coarse rock salt or sea salt whenever there is enough time for the grains to dissolve properly, and for the same reason I use as fine salt as possible for the final seasoning of a dish.

I am one of those cooks who believe that light meat, most vegetables and sauces require white pepper, while black pepper is best for red meat and dark sauces, and that both should be freshly ground, straight from the mill.

The false morel, *(Gyromitra esculenta)*, a highly valued mushroom in Finnish eyes, is beginning to be a rarity in other parts of the world. It is still a fairly common commercial species in Finland, however, although its sale has been restricted in many European countries in recent years on account of its extreme toxicity. If processed and prepared with care, it is wonderfully tasty, e.g. when chopped and fried and served in a cream sauce with spring salmon or whitefish.

To remove the poison, boil the mushrooms carefully in at least two changes of water, for at least 5 minutes each time, throwing the water away immediately (as this will also be poisonous!) and rinsing the mushrooms well after each boiling. If you are boiling a large number of these mushrooms at one time, make sure that the kitchen is well ventilated, as a certain amount of the toxin will evaporate in the steam. The best way of preserving false morels is to dry them thoroughly without boiling, and then to boil them twice in the same manner as above immediately before using them.

It is also possible to replace these false morels with the morel *(Morchella esculenta)*, which is rarely available fresh but easy to find preserved, and is even of very much the same appearance.

Weights, Measures & Temperatures

Weights

1 pound (lb) = 16 ounces = 453.6 grams (g)
1 ounce (oz.) = 28.35 g
1 kilogram (kg) = 1000 g = 2 lbs 3 oz.
100 g = 3.5 oz.

Measures

1 US gallon = 4 liquid quarts = 3.785 litres (l)
1 liquid quart = 2 liquid pints = 9.5 decilitres (dl)
1 liquid pint = 16 US fl. oz. = 4.73 dl
1 cup = 8 US oz. = 29.6 millilitres (ml)
1 quart (dry) = 1.1 litres
1 litre = 10 dl = (more than) 2 pints
1 decilitre = (less than) 1/2 cup

Temperatures

Fahrenheit	Centigrade
268°F	131°C
350°F	177°C
375-400°F	190-204°C
450-500°F	232-260°C

Centigrade	Fahrenheit
100°C	212°F
200°C	392°F
250°C	482°F
300°C	572°F

Selyanka and Vorschmack explained

Selyanka (Russ.) a soup based on fish (usually salmon), chicken or beef and typically flavoured with green olives, capers, pickled cucumbers, tomato puré and lemon.

Vorschmack (Germ.) a herring and meat casserole baked in the oven, of presumably Jewish-Polish-Baltic-Swedish origin. The name means a foretaste.

Field-Marshal Mannerheim's vorschmack was made of minced herring together with finely minced lamb and veal, onion and garlic. It is mostly served nowadays with baked potatoes and sour cream.

This is certainly not what we would call a fast food, as it has to be cooked for a full two days.

Our warmest thanks go to the following people for their help, the loan of materials and access to beautiful scenes for the photographs.

Jan de la Chapelle, owner of the Lindö Manor House, Tenhola

Björn Björklöf, fisherman, Barösund

Jara Farm, catering suppliers, Lempäälä

Maarit Timonen, stallholder, Helsinki Market Place

Kivikopla Oy, Espoo

Stockmann, Helsinki department store

All our excellent suppliers of fresh ingredients

In particular we would like to thank our friend Maria Planting and the staff of E. Ahlström Oy for their cooperation and for the dishes and cutlery that we were able to use for the illustrations. We also rely on their style and quality in everyday use at the Helsinki Culinary Institute and at Villa Hakkari.

The Authors

And last but by no means least, I would like to thank my colleagues at the Helsinki Culinary Institute and Villa Hakkari for their patience and for all the help they have given to the authors of this book.

Gero

Sources

Michel Jamais
Vin & Gastronomi
Millhouse Förlag, 2001

Larousse Gastronomique
Hamlyn, 1999

Risto ja Ritva Lehmusoksa
Mannerheimin pöydässä
Gummerus Oy
Ajatus Kirjat, 2003

Eero Mäkelä, Gero Hottinger, Pekka Immonen
New Flavours from Finland
Muikkutortusta riekonrintaan
Otava Publishing Co., 2003

Juha Tanttu
Ah, Savoy
Siis Savoy
Otava Publishing Co., 1997

Ville Vallgren
Pariisin Villen Ruokasaarna
Suom. Kyllikki Villa
Kustannusosakeyhtiö Taide, 1994

Werner Vögeli
Från Emmental till Stockholms Slott
Bokförlaget Prisma, 2003

Index to the recipes

Starters

Asparagus with puff pastries and orange zabaglione
12

Smoked Baltic herring salad
18

Soufflé of potato, boletus mushrooms and quark
25

Finnish charr au bleu
14

Vegetable terrine with fresh tomato sauce
20

Smoked reindeer with baked turnip
26

Plaited herring with a sour cream and apple sauce
16

Warm chanterelle salad and balsámico syrup
22

Sweet & sour Baltic herrings
29

Whitefish tartare flavoured with gin
17

Duck's liver hamburger
24

Pasta and crayfish tails in Finlandia Vodka and cream sauce
31

Soups

Salmon and scallop carpaccio
32

Ville Vallgren's salmon soup
36

Boletus soup
41

Finnish strawberries Italian style
34

Summer cucumber soup
38

Gero's sauerkraut soup
42

Beetroot and basil soup
39

Pork sausage soup
flavoured with saffron
43

Sweet pepper and tomato soup with
goat's cheese
40

Fish courses

Spring pike in
cucumber and mustard sauce
46

Fillets of perch with mushroom,
sweetbread and crayfish stuffing
50

Fried fillet of pike-perch, ratatouille
and rosemary sauce
58

Summer whitefish
with butter sauce
47

Perch steaks filled with spinach
51

Pike-perch Mediterranean style
60

Whitefish cooked whole in foil
48

Fried pike-perch
Mannerheim-style
56

Fried flounder with
dill and crayfish filling
61

Smoked fillet of whitefish with
butter sauce and new potatoes
49

Pike-perch oriental style
57

Quick salmon quenelles
in champagne sauce
62

Something green

False morel and salmon sandwich
with hollandaise sauce
64

Vendace deep fried
in a beer dough
68

Spinach cakes
with watercress sauce
72

Salmon, kohlrabi and basil froth
65

Fillet of burbot
with lemon-grass sauce
69

Chanterelle and
spring cabbage rolls
73

Tomato and ginger herrings
66

Apple rings coated with sesame seeds
and served with honey sauce
74

Casseroled vendace
67

Meat dishes

Entrecôte steaks with
stone pine seeds and pistachios
78

Lamb chops with goat's cheese,
ratatouille and rosemary sauce
86

Whole roast wild duck
with redcurrant sauce
96

Veal noisettes with green asparagus
and hollandaise sauce
79

Roast lamb with beans,
French style
88

Wild duck with apple and
calvados sauce
98

Fried liver and steamed fennel
with coriander sauce
80

Turkey saltimbocca
89

Breast of willow grouse with
white truffle and boletus sauce
99

Fillet of pork with beer sauce
81

Breast of wood pigeon
with creamed savoy cabbage
90

Breast of duck with
a potato cake and French beans
100

Recipes

Desserts

Fillet of reindeer
with endive and madeira sauce
104

Apple pastries with raspberry sauce
114

Caramel custard with cloudberries
119

Fillet of reindeer, juniper berry
sauce and potato and boletus hash
105

Orange cheesecake
115

A dessert trio
120

Elk Wallenbergare
107

Rhubarb tiramisu
116

The best quark tart
of my childhood days
124

Elk meat goulash with spätzle
108

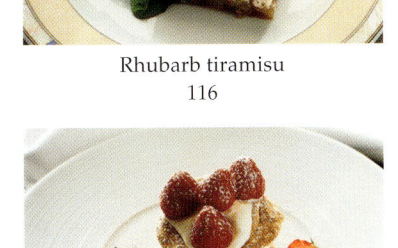

Strawberry surprise
117

Chocolate expresso fondant
125

Summer berry tart
118

© 2004 Gero Hottinger and Otava Publishing Company

Photographs: Kaj G. Lindholm
Text and Editing: Pekka Råman
Translation: Malcolm Hicks
Graphic Design: Jaakko Mäkikylä, Riitta Skytt/Meridian X Oy

Printed by Otava Book Printing Company Ltd.
Keuruu 2004
ISBN 951-1-19785-1